Up the Inlet

Copyright © 2015 Wayne J. Lutz

All rights reserved. No part of this publication may be reproduced, stored in a retrieval system, or transmitted, in any form or by any means, electronic, mechanical, photocopying, recording, or otherwise, without the written prior permission of the author. Reviewers are authorized to quote short passages within a book review, as permitted under the United States Copyright Act of 1976.

Note for Librarians: a catalog record for this book that includes Dewey Decimal Classification and U.S. Library of Congress numbers is available from the Library and Archives of Canada. The complete catalog record can be obtained from their online database at:
www.collectionscanada.ca/amicus/index-e.html

ISBN 978-1-927438-11-4
Printed in the United States of America

Powell River Books
Powell RIver, BC
Book sales online at:
www.powellriverbooks.com
phone: 604-483-1704
email: wlutz@mtsac.edu

10 9 8 7 6 5 4 3 2 1

Up the Inlet
Coastal British Columbia Stories

Wayne J. Lutz

2015
Powell River Books

*The stories are true, and the characters are real.
Some details are adjusted to protect the guilty.
All of the mistakes rest solidly with the author.*

Front Cover Photo:
 Forbes Bay, Homfray Channel (north of Desolation Sound)

Back Cover Photos:
 Top: Theodosia Inlet at Sunrise (looking northeast)
 Bottom: Departing Powell River's North Harbour

Other Books by Wayne J. Lutz

Coastal British Columbia Stories
Up the Lake
Up the Main
Up the Winter Trail
Up the Strait
Up the Airway
Farther Up the Lake
Farther Up the Main
Farther Up the Strait
Cabin Number 5
Off the Grid

Science Fiction Titles
Across the Galactic Sea
Echo of a Distant Planet
Inbound to Earth
When Galazies Collide

www.PowellRiverBooks.com

Up the Inlet

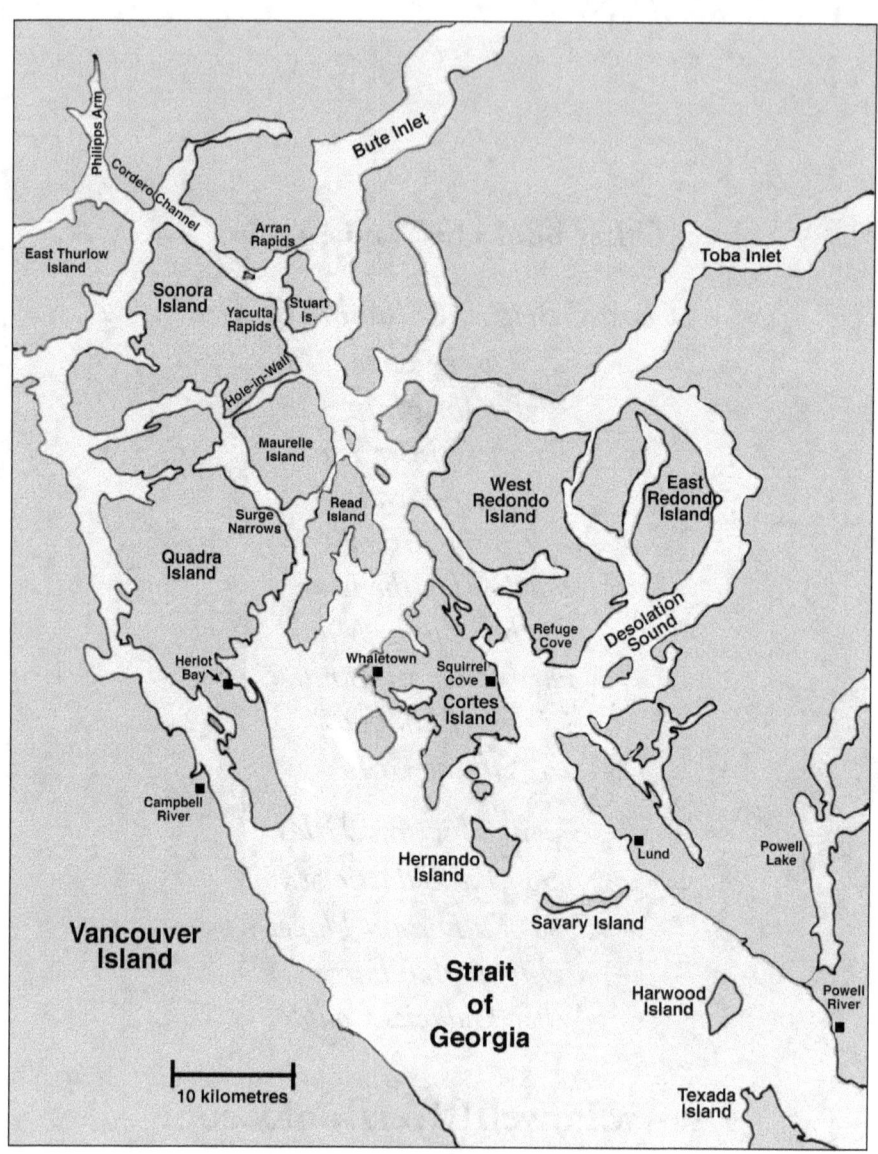

Regional Overview

Wayne J. Lutz

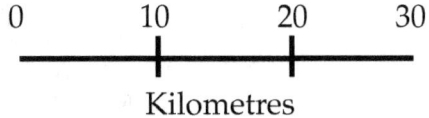

Lower Coastal
British Columbia

Up the Inlet

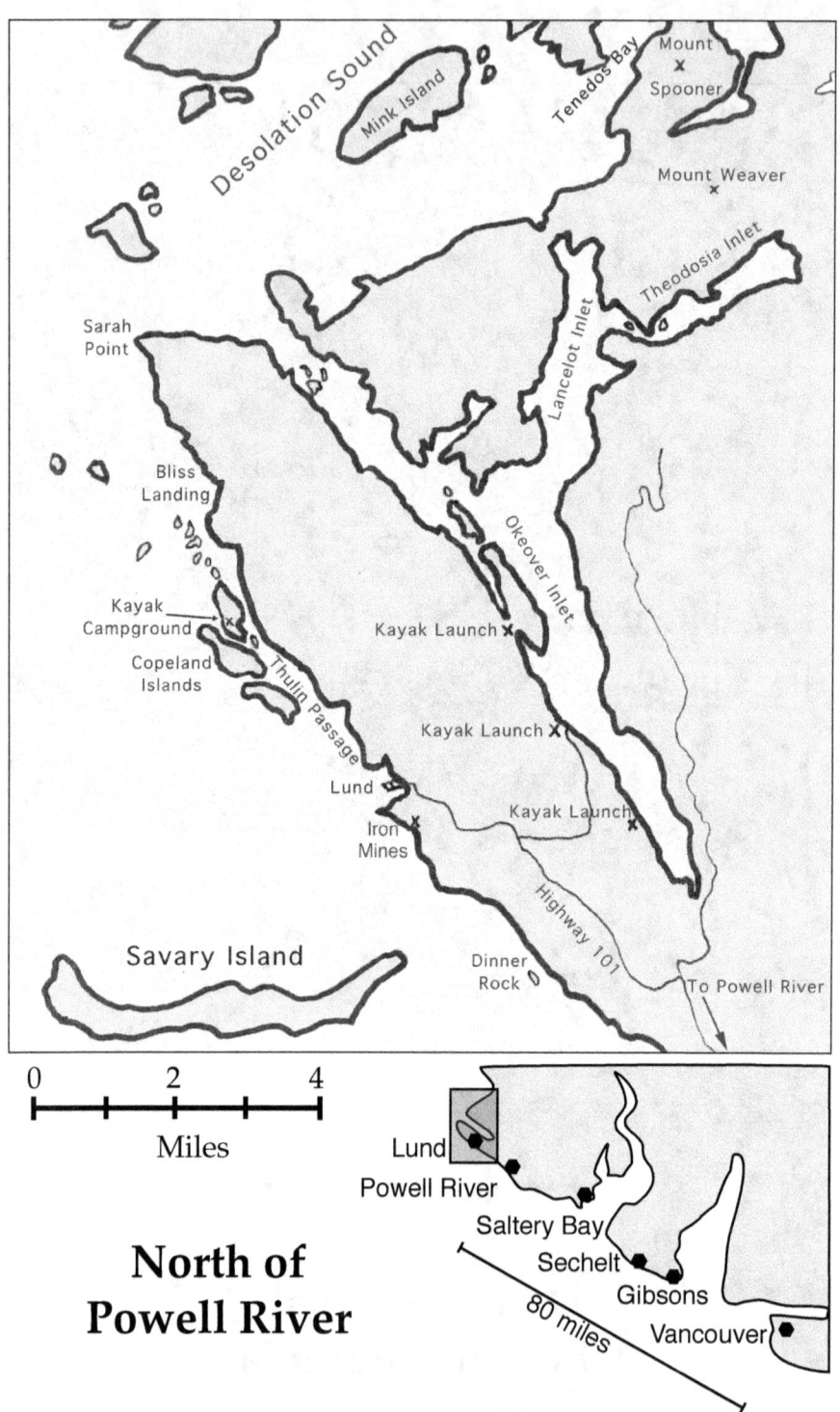

North of Powell River

Contents

Preface – Straits and Inlets 10
1 – Return to Mitlenatch 12
2 – Down the Inlet 21
3 – Solo 33
4 – The Imperfect Boat 50
5 – Boat Shopping 68
6 – Anchor Freefall 84
7 – North to Powell River 94
8 – Zincs and Wheelbarrows 108
9 – Downrigger Rookie 115
10 – First Trip North 122
11 – The Tides of Washington 140
12 - Flower Rocks 150
13 - Boat Island 166
14 - Too Big to Fail 182
Epilogue – Inlets and More Inlets 204
Geographic Index 206
About the Author 209

Prologue

Straits and Inlets

After writing the original *Up the Strait*, I was convinced I needed to travel farther north to the coastal destinations of historic lore. After all, if I wrote another book about boating on the coastline of BC, it should cover new destinations, distant from the Strait of Georgia. Yet I loved the places I kept returning to right in my own backyard, seldom venturing past the northern end of Cortes and Quadra Island. But I wanted to write about the real notables of the north, like the Broughton Archipelago and Knight Inlet. Places in coastal history like Minstrel Island and Kingcome Inlet.

Closer to home, the northern Strait of Georgia spreads out to sublime destinations, including Desolation Sound and its famous Inlets – Okeover, Lancelot, and Theodosia. But as majestic as these places might be, they weren't distant enough to make my boating adventures complete.

In *Farther Up the Strait*, I began with ambitions to travel to new docks and anchorages, and I did. But I didn't travel very far. I kept returning to the beauty of Mitlenatch, Rebecca Spit, Von Donop Inlet, and all the locations I cherished. These spectacular places were within a day's travel of Powell River, which made them even more enticing. Still, I had an excuse to stay close to home, since an unused book title lingered on the distant drawing boards – *Up the Inlet*.

This is that book, and my chance to carry readers to the havens I hoped to visit from the very beginning. It will be an opportunity to explore farther north with *Halcyon Days*, the 24-foot Bayliner I've always referred to as "the perfect boat." She's a trusty vessel (with an admittedly fickle motor), although barely big enough to weather the seas when conditions get rough. She has only a single engine and isn't comfortable in waves greater than a metre, but I can control that by traveling with one eye on the weather and my other eye on the engine temperature gauge.

John, my mentor and friend, keeps at me: "You need a bigger boat, at least 28-feet, twin-engines, and a dinghy that isn't a safety hazard." (I beg your pardon, *Mr. Bathtub* – you've been a integral part of my adventures.) How could I ever part with a boat as precious as *Halcyon Days*?

It's winter now, but that brings dreams of warm sun and boating on the chuck. *Halcyon Days* will travel north, and I'll finally be able to write about the mythical destinations that have been the source of my dreams – the grand inlets of the north. Unless, of course, John somehow talks me into a bigger boat. Or, more likely, I can't break away from the beauty of my favourite places closer to home.

Often, great adventures are spawned by dreams never attained. The deviations along the way – what I call "unexpected destinations" – can be part of life's grand joys. Sometimes it's best to simply set sail, and see what happens.

Chapter 1

Return to Mitlenatch

Mitlenatch has become a regular stop in my journeys up and down the Strait of Georgia. Usually, this island requires only a minor course deviation, so it attracts me again and again. In fact, on some voyages, I find myself having to navigate around Mitlenatch just to get to where I'm going. So why not stop?

On a two-day cruise to Quadra Island's Rebecca Spit, Mitlenatch is directly along our path. Since Margy and I are anxious to get to the fuel dock at Heriot Bay before it closes, we bypass the island by a few kilometres. But we know we'll want to visit Mitlenatch on our return.

This early-June trip is during a period when we're coming off an unusually cool spring, and this is one of the first sunny days. When we arrive at Heriot Bay, we find the marina very quiet, a victim of the prolonged marginal weather coupled with a global economy that's still shaking from the rumbles of a prolonged downturn. Now, two years after the financial crisis first surfaced, the boating economy is going through aftershocks further hampered by a strong loonie that brings fewer Americans to these waters. A good way to judge the impact is to stop for fuel almost anywhere on the coast. Today, the normal waiting lines are non-existent.

The hotel deck is basking in the late afternoon sun, making a fine venue for an early dinner. As much fun as it is to prepare meals aboard *Halcyon Days*, supper with a paid cook and dishwasher simplifies a one-nighter.

After dining on the patio, we depart Heriot Bay, and swing around the buoy that marks the rocky ledge near the ferry terminal. Drew Harbour, adjacent to Rebecca Spit, is a favourite anchorage for boaters during the summer, but it's nearly vacant today.

Inside Rebecca Spit at Drew Harbour

A large crew-boat-style vessel is pulled up onto the beach. Otherwise the area is empty except for the boats docked at the resort on the west side of the bay and the residences to the south.

I let out lots of rode in 20-feet of water and then secure the anchor, with plenty of room to swing between here and shore as the tide rises. Meanwhile, a few people appear on the spit near the crew boat. They get aboard quickly, and head back to the resort on the other side of the bay.

"Tourons!" proclaims Margy.

Undoubtedly true. There aren't a lot of tourists here today, but at least there are some. The sun is bright, and will be with us all the way to the almost-flat horizon to the northwest. Days are nearly as long as they get, and this one is sunny and warm.

Before sunset, two cruisers join us in the anchorage, three boats in an area that can easily hold twenty or more. For some reason, they tuck in fairly close to us, maybe because they assume we know the best place to anchor. Meanwhile, the rest of the bay remains empty.

Empty, that is, until the locals arrive. A sporty runabout maneuvers between our three boats, speeding past as if this is a buoy-marked course. The red-and-white speedboat zips past, passengers waving and stirring up quite a wake. Normally, this would be considered a major indiscretion in an anchorage, but there's something acutely funny when the bay is wide open except for three anchored boats. Maybe it's a friendly way for the locals to say "Hello." I wave back, then brace myself for the wake.

The young boaters head for the south side, where they drop down off-plane and come to a stop. In a few minutes, they're accelerating again, this time pulling a wake-boarder and headed our way. Once again, they maneuver between the only anchored boats in the bay. The wake-boarder gives a friendly wave, and I wave back. Somehow, this absurdity marks a pleasant introduction to summer, when speedboats like this will be a more clearly-defined nuisance. For now, it's an enjoyable proclamation: "Summer's here!"

Later that night, a man and a woman in a <u>very</u> small boat putt-putt through our three-vessel flotilla. The boat is as small as our dinghy, *Mr. Bathtub*, and has the same minimal freeboard. But it isn't from one of the boats anchored nearby. The tiny craft executes a zigzag course around our group, and then heads back to the south side of the bay. There's definitely something traditional here about how the locals herald the arrival of summer at Rebecca Spit.

In fact, the next morning, as we're preparing to raise anchor, another small boat swings through the area. This time it's a red tin boat with a three-person crew: man, woman, and dog. They swing gently between the three anchored boats, and then back home to the south. The big black dog, as is typical, enthusiastically surveys the scene from his precarious perch in the bow.

Later in the morning, as we exit the harbour, we see Mitlenatch Island as soon as we swing around the headland of the spit. "So near, yet so far" is a fitting description of the island, which seems to float in the diffuse boundary between sea and sky. As we get closer, Mitlenatch doesn't seem to be growing in size, reminding me of another saying about the mysterious locale: "The closer you get, the farther it seems." And it's true – we've traveled at least 10 kilometres, and the island seems no closer.

Tin boat at Drew Harbour

The tide is low, and the sea is nearly calm. We pass through an area of surface seaweed, slowing momentarily to make sure our prop doesn't pick up any debris. Farther ahead, several distinct dark ovals

Approaching Mitlenatch

Mitlenatch Island

promise more of the same. As we draw closer to the next patch, I prepare to come back on the throttle, but then I notice that it isn't seaweed at all. Instead, it's simply an area where the wind has rustled up ripples on the surface, so we stay on-plane and pass on through.

This is the area of the upper Strait of Georgia where the tides meet, flowing in from the south and also down from the north along the inside of Vancouver Island. The mixing here produces unusual tidal conditions and some of the warmest water in the region. Mitlenatch itself is desert-like compared to its surroundings, sitting in the rain shadow of Vancouver Island. No wonder Mitlenatch is considered the Galapagos of the Strait of Georgia.

I slow to idle about a kilometre from the island, a lot earlier than I normally would decelerate as I approach land. I do this in respect for the plentiful marine life, a small price to pay for the privilege of visiting an island of abundant birds, sea animals, and bountiful wildflowers.

A sailboat is anchored in Northwest Bay, with two kayaks now leaving shore and headed towards us as we approach. By the time our anchor is down, the kayaks are aboard the sailboat, and we'll soon be alone in the bay.

Holding conditions in this location are described in our boating guide as "relatively poor." So this should only be a day hook, meant for times like this, when sea conditions are smooth and shore visits are brief. I provide plenty of scope for the anchor in 30 feet of water, and we wait 15 minutes to assure we're not dragging. Then I prepare *Mr. Bathtub* for the short trip to shore.

"Wear your shoes," I tell Margy. "I'll wear my water slippers, and pull you and *Mr. Bathtub* up to shore so your feet won't get wet."

"I can wear my water shoes," she replies.

But I'm worried she'll sprain an ankle during the hike on-shore, something that plagues her and always requires consideration. So I insist she wear her regular shoes.

By the time we maneuver *Mr. Bathtub* close to the shingle beach, it's obvious that my advice was in error. We become bogged down on a sharp, rocky bottom in the still ebbing tide. I get out of the dinghy and try to pull Margy in closer to shore, but *Mr. Bathtub* grinds on the rocks.

"I guess you'll need to get out," I say. "But don't ruin your shoes in the salt water. Take them off and leave your socks on because of the rocks."

It's the best idea possible, now that I've put us in this corner. It's not a pleasant trek for Margy over the rocks in her socks.

We carry the dinghy up the gravel beach, hoisting *Mr. Bathtub* high enough to be satisfied it will still be here when we return. Margy puts her shoes back on (over wet socks), and we hike along the narrow path that leads up towards the bird blind at the top of the cliff. Behind me, as we begin the climb, I can hear Margy's shoes squishing as they still spurt out water. As we climb higher, Glaucous-winged gulls squawk continuously as we get closer to their nesting area near the top.

These giant birds are covered in more stark-white feathers than most gulls. They take over this island in the spring, along with the resident sea lions and a mix of breathtaking wildflowers. Some flowers remain today, but most have already begun to go to seed. We're a few weeks late for the wildflower bloom that covers this island in the heart of spring.

I hike increasingly ahead of Margy, who stops often to investigate the remaining flowers and take some photos. This is a narrow trail, like the many other paths on the island, and initially, it seems difficult to

Approaching Bird Blind

navigate. But it maintains its barely-open width all the way to the top where the bird blind overlooks the cliff.

At the wooden blind, I sit on the narrow bench and peer through the slit-like opening in the wall. Glaucous-winged gulls are spread all

Glaucous-Winged Gull

along the top of the cliff, each claiming their own territory from the nearly continuous blanket of birds. Occasionally, the male of a pair of gulls goes airborne for a brief flight that brings him back down to the same spot next to his mate, with an undercurrent of squawks from his neighbors: "Watch out, this is my territory!"

Margy joins me now in the bird blind, and we spend some quite time together, whispering about what we see, trying not to interfere with the gulls that sit only a few metres in front of us.

When we hike back down to the beach, Margy stops and snaps a photo of *Halcyon Days* bobbing on her anchor in Northwest Bay. The sea is barely rippled, and Campbell River is visible in the distance. Our boat, like the island as we approached it, seems so near, yet so far. It's a magical place.

Back down at the beach, Margy and I formulate our plan for getting *Mr. Bathtub* back in the water. I suggest we carry the boat to the boulder area to the east where we can get closer to the water without trudging over the smaller slimy rocks. It's a longer carry, but with fewer obstacles than hauling the dinghy down the slippery slope of the beach.

Bayliner anchored in Northwest Bay

It's not as easy a route as I expected, but finally we're back in the water. In only a few hours, we've entered Northwest Bay, explored the lushest region of the island (at least of the portion open to visitors), and we're now on our way home. Mitlenatch is one of the most-easily accessible splendors of the northern edge of the Strait of Georgia, and we'll come here again and again to enjoy its natural glories. So close to home, yet so far.

Margy with *Mr. Bathtub*; Bayliner in background

◊ ◊ ◊ ◊ ◊ ◊ ◊

Chapter 2

Down the Inlet

After another fine summer of cruising the chuck in the local area, the inlets to the north are still in my dreams. Once again, I've visited my favourite spots at the expense of a long trip to the Broughton Archipelago and its classic inlets. There are plenty of excuses, most of them related to my enchantment with my floating cabin on Powell Lake. To leave home in the midst of summer is a difficult decision. It's not easy to break away from the lake, where my personal call of the sirens provides a mesmerizing aura. So I remain on the lake, occasionally venturing out on the chuck for cruises of a few days at a time.

Along the southern BC coast, "up the inlet" almost universally means a trip north. Sechelt Inlet is the exception, with its orientation southward from its entrance near Egmont. Narrows and Salmon Inlet branch off to the east. Both of these arms are major voyages in themselves.

At the head of Sechelt Inlet (the <u>south</u> end) is Porpoise Bay and the town of Sechelt, situated on the narrow strip of land separating the head of the inlet from the Strait of Georgia. A canal connecting the two has been proposed and repeatedly rejected, so the town remains a port for the head of the tranquil inlet, rather than a harbour for the busy Strait of Georgia side of the isthmus.

On a summer day, John and Bro (his trusty Labrador retriever) accompany Margy and me to a beach near Porpoise Bay. *Mr. Kayak* rides atop our Ford Tempo, after a one-ferry ride south from Powell River. Near the shore, we organize our gear on a grassy area, adjacent to a sign declaring: "No Dogs on the Beach." Then we carry the kayak to the shore for a day trip "down" the inlet (northward, in this case). Contrary to all of our other inlet voyages, we were entering from its head, rather than from the mouth.

Ignoring the "No Dogs" sign, Bro provides a few last-minute barks as Margy and I paddle away. Our plan is to meet at a haul-out spot near the end of the road that parallels the shore as it winds northward.

In light winds and almost no tidal current, we paddle past elaborate waterfront homes. The head of this inlet is a far cry from the isolation of Toba or Bute, but it provides a nice day of easy paddling. As we approach our prearranged pull-out spot before Nine Mile Point and the entrance to Salmon Inlet, John and Bro were waiting impatiently on the shore. It hasn't been a lengthy voyage to remote reaches, but there'll be other opportunities to explore farther up (and down) this inlet with our Bayliner.

* * * * *

A FEW MONTHS LATER, APPROACHING the fuel dock at Egmont in Halcyon Days, the water stirs strangely. Now near low tide, the rush of water at nearby Skookumchuck still churns the marina. I maneuver the Bayliner towards the dock, but it's an awkward approach. I back away and try again. The fuel attendant appears near the pumps, ready to grab my lines.

"It's the dreaded 90-degree approach," I yell from the command bridge, as I try to catch the drift better this time. "Water moves strange here."

"That it does," replies the attendant, matter-of-factly. I can tell by his smile that he's used to watching amateurs struggling at this dock.

I back away again. This time I achieve a reasonable 45-degree approach. On this try, it actually looks like I know what I'm doing. We glide nicely towards the fuel pumps. The attendant grabs the Bayliner's forward rail before the current can pull us away from the dock again. He helps secure our lines, and hands me the gas hose.

"Quiet today," I observe.

"Summer's over," replies the attendant. He looks relieved.

The fuel dock is nearly vacant. It's September 6th, only two days after Labour Day, but the calendar says back-to-school. The southern BC coast has almost instantly transformed itself from a bustling tourist

Egmont Marina

destination to a laid-back atmosphere. Today is sunny and warm, no different from the previous weekend. But the level of activity is completely different.

Climbing the steep ramp to shore, Margy and I pause and survey the marina and its majestic backdrop. I look down into the clear water. Immediately below the ramp is a perfect natural exhibit of various species of starfish, barely submerged in the low tide. Several five-armed, purple Pacific Starfish rest next to a bright orange Sunflower Star (with twenty legs!). A few feet closer to shore, an orange, web-footed Bat Star clings to a rock. It's like an exhibit in a marine museum.

Today we're headed "down the inlet" – no, it's "up the inlet," south towards the head at Sechelt. The feel, however, is distinctly "down." Accompanying today's "down the inlet" mystique are the tide tables, which leave me baffled. I carry copies of the flow schedule for Egmont and Porpoise Bay, printed from the Internet last night. I also have an up-to-date BC boater's guide with this year's tides, but I don't have the official Canadian government tide tables for this area. My two sources of data differ by a only a few minutes between stations; yet they list the approaching low tide at Egmont and Porpoise Bay as nearly three hours apart. Three hours difference in less than 30 kilometres. It seems impossible.

Concerned by this disparity, I'd prefer another tide table for comparison. I expect Egmont Marina to have the standard posted-on-the-door local tidal numbers, with copies of the official Canadian tables available in the marina store. Except, it's no longer summer (by a mere few days), so there's no data available.

Correction – there is data, but it's last weekend's information. On the door to the store is the expected grease-marker posting. The whiteboard has three columns of tide information. The last column is for September 4th, the day summer ended. The store's last copy of the Canadian tide tables has been sold. Now that summer is over, I guess there are no tides.

We walk up to the Wilderness Lodge. I visualize what this place looked like two days ago. Today there are only two cars in the parking lot. Housekeeping workers leisurely push carts down the sidewalk, still cleaning up from the holiday weekend onslaught. In the restaurant, we're the only customers.

But there's an up-to-date tide schedule for Skookumchuck on the whiteboard outside the gift shop. I compare these times to a tide reminder note I'm carrying in my backpack. The posted Skookumchuck current maximums are appropriately between those of Egmont and Porpoise Bay, so now I feel more confident the times I have are accurate. But still there are significant differences between Egmont, Skookumchuck, and Sechelt. I'm used to a few minutes variation over such short distances, rather than almost three hours. Skookumchuck Rapids boasts the strongest flow rates in coastal BC (16 knots), so I shouldn't be surprised by these large tidal variations.

We return to *Halcyon Days*, and get ready to depart. We'll pass through Skookumchuck twenty minutes before slack tide, and turns out to be a smooth journey. There are a few swirls and crosscurrents still evident, but we power through smoothly in slow cruise.

The GPS keeps us oriented, and we slip past the most critical spot, Roland Point, where I've watched swift-water kayaks from the shoreline during the middle of summer – small, blunt-nose vessels riding the huge standing waves before a crowd of spectators. Today the shore is deserted, partly because it's slack tide, and partly because summer has been declared over.

With Skookumchuck behind us, it's quiet water all the way past Narrows Inlet to the mouth of Salmon Inlet. Here the afternoon wind churns the waves, and it's rough all the way across the arm's mouth. It seems obvious that the far side of Salmon Inlet should be smoother, since it's on the lee side of the mountains.

At the inlet, we turn left and motor up the fjord-like passage in slightly improved conditions. Here the usual north orientation (actually northeast) is restored. We're going up the inlet in the normal direction again. I expect some inflow winds in Salmon Inlet, but they turn out to be minimal.

Passing Black Bear Point, the waves smooth even further to a light chop. I scan closely for bears, since it looks like the perfect place, but I see none.

We continue up the inlet to the head, where we stop mid-channel to view the large powerplant and logging camp. It's not a busy spot, but Misery Bay, now behind us, seems more appropriate for an overnight anchorage. So we return down the inlet to the small bay and drop anchor in 40 feet of water.

Near our anchorage, a logging road runs down to a dock where a classic old red-and-green trawler is moored. Its captain, who I assume is a resident in this spot, motors back and forth in his tin boat during early evening, checking his crab traps.

A seemingly lonely seal swims in the bay, which seems indicative of fish. I drop my line over the side, and jig near the bottom. Almost immediately, I catch two small rockfish. Then the fishing goes from feverish to nothing more.

Other than the old trawler, we're the only boat in Misery Bay. I'm sure this contrasts markedly with the high level of activity the previous weekend. Everywhere we travel, the message is the same – summer is obviously over.

* * * * *

THE NEXT MORNING, BEFORE SUNRISE, I sit on the aft deck. Seals pop to the surface in the predawn murkiness. They swim in groups of four or five, a scene that reminds me of synchronized swimmers demonstrating their skills. Seals converge on a common point until they're only a few metres apart. Then they split off in different directions. It reminds me of an Esther Williams aquatic ballet. Or, better yet, a Snowbirds aerial flight display.

After a few minutes, all of the seals disappear, underwater or gone from the bay. I feel more comfortable fishing now, since I've no desire to hook a seal. I drop my line, and almost immediately catch two more rockfish on back-to-back casts.

At 9 am, I begin securing the cabin in preparation for raising anchor. It will be wise to beat the clock-like inflow winds that are probably brewing at the mouth of the inlet. I use the narrow catwalk to climb around the cabin from the aft deck to the bow. Then, kneeling near the anchor winch, I prepare to raise the hook.

The sound of a helicopter grows from the south, so I pause to see what happens. In a few minutes, a green-and-white Bell JetRanger zooms in low, overflies the bay, and drops even lower for its approach to the logging dock. It lands near the dirt road, adjacent to the old trawler, in a cloud of dust.

While the rotor still whirls, two red-vested workers exit the helicopter. The Jet Ranger waits for them to clear the arc of the rotor, before powering up in increasing dust. It lifts off and veers straight towards us – Greetings, Bayliner! As the helicopter roars overhead, I wave from the bow. The Jet Ranger banks sharply to the north, and is upward and onward on its morning rounds.

* * * * *

WE MAKE IT DOWN SALMON INLET before the inflow winds arrive. I maneuver the Bayliner to the left and southward towards Porpoise Bay. We'll need to refuel at the head of the inlet, and our boating guide indicates gas is available only at the Tofino Air seaplane base. It seems strange that a marina as large as Porpoise Bay doesn't have fuel, but we'll know for sure when we stop for lunch.

Porpoise Bay is a disappointment. There's no space available at the public wharf, and the motel marina also looks tight. But we find a spot on the motel dock and get approval to leave our boat for an hour.

When we walk to the Lighthouse Inn for lunch, we find it closed until noon. That's only another half-hour, but I'm impatient and ready to leave. We confirm there's no fuel here, so I telephone Tofino Air to confirm the availability of gas at their marina.

We depart Porpoise Bay after only a 15-minute visit and no lunch. It's a short ride to the combined seaplane base and marina, just a few kilometres to the north – a fascinating place.

Initially, I pull into the wrong gas pumps. Once I hop onto the dock, it's obvious these are the avgas pumps. Margy stays on the dock, while I swing around to the other side, past three floatplanes: a powerful Turbo Otter, a Beaver with a classic radial engine, and a Cessna 180.

By the time I'm nestled in beside the Cessna, the fuel attendant has arrived from the onshore office. He's young, enthusiastic, and a candidate for aviation talk.

"Are you planning to learn to fly?" I ask. Somehow he looks prime for the task. I've worked with budding young aviators for decades, and he has that determined look.

"I've already had my first lesson with the Air Cadets, but it's tough to find an airplane for instruction here," he replies.

Tofino Air Marina, Sechelt

He doesn't seem surprised at my question, nor do I explain how I knew he's a budding student pilot. Inwardly, I'm proud I was able to identify his occupational profile at first glance. On the other hand, I've watched line-boys at airports for decades, and they wouldn't be there unless they loved airplanes. Of course, technically, this is a boat marina as much as a seaplane base.

"Was your lesson in a seaplane?" I ask.

"No, I flew in a Cessna 152 at the Sechelt Airport. But the airplane isn't insured for flight instruction, and there's nothing here that will work. I'm thinking of going to Nanaimo for flying lessons."

That will be tough. I visualize how he'll require two ferries and an all-day drive to get to Nanaimo. For the next few minutes, we discuss Air Cadet Robert's plans for an aviation career. As a U.S. flight instructor, I try to discourage him from thoughts of buying a training airplane and hiring an independent instructor.

"I know it sounds economically feasible, but it isn't," I try to explain. "The purchase price of an airplane is the smallest part of the expense of ownership."

I could explain to Robert in detail regarding the pitfalls of this learn-to-fly path, but I decide to leave it alone. If Margy and I can help Robert find a better route to his pilot's licence, that's the best way to prevent him from sinking his hard-earned money into an airplane. Especially at his age, aircraft ownership would be an endless money pit. I'm totally convinced of this, but I know youth, and I know my arguments might be wasting my breath.

"We're both pilots," offers Margy. "We're members of a flying club in Powell River, and we're currently trying to arrange flight lessons for student pilots. It's a lot closer than Nanaimo."

Why didn't I think of that? Margy is right – the Westview Flying Club is trying to get a flight instructor to come to Powell River from Courtney. In our ferry-isolated community, it's difficult to arrange flying lessons. For this young student pilot, Powell River is a lot closer than Nanaimo, one ferry ride rather than two.

Margy walks back to the Tofino Air office with Robert to settle our fuel bill. I'm fearful that our flying club's plans for a flight school at Powell River will not be realized, but it seems the best solution for Robert.

"Nice kid," says Margy when she returns to the boat. "I hope we can help him."

But it isn't to be. Powell River's plans for an on-site flight school ends before it gets off the ground, a victim of the floundering aviation economy. We've lost contact with Robert since then, but I know young fellows like him persevere, so it's not unlikely that he's already flying professionally. Fly high and fast, Robert.

* * * * *

HEADING NORTH FROM OUR GAS STOP, we pass Salmon Inlet, and then pause at the entrance to Narrows Inlet to troll for salmon. I've never had any luck trolling, except when fishing for trout in lake environments. But this is prime salmon territory, and this inlet looks like the perfect spot.

We start slowly up Narrows Inlet, killing time as we wait for the 2:37 pm turn of the tide at Tzoonie Narrows. I follow the 400-foot-depth contour on the GPS. It's not serious salmon fishing, since I'm a whatever-happens fisherman, with crimped barbs on my lure. I estimate the lure is riding 50 feet deep on its Deep-6 trolling rig. Even if I surprise myself with a salmon, I plan to release it. After all, if I keep it, I'll have to kill it first. But I'd sure like to catch one. That doesn't happen today. After passing an elaborate floating cabin on the starboard shore, I pull in my fishing line. We throttle up for the rest of the ride up the inlet.

We arrive at Tzoonie Narrows near slack water. This is one of the inspiring spots from Muriel Wylie Blanchet's *Curve of Time*. I can't help but think of this historic book as we pass through the channel. Narrows Inlet, with its mountainous sidewalls, rises even more dramatically than Salmon Inlet. In Tzoonie Narrows, it's especially spectacular.

At the head of Narrows Inlet, we find a wide, scenic bay that reminds me of the head of Hotham Sound. It's the perfect anchorage, and only one other boat (the size and shape of our Bayliner) floats nearby. We drop anchor near the Tzoonie River delta in 30 feet of water.

This is a comfortable spot, with shallow depths near the mud flats. Steep vertical walls on each side of the wide-open inlet thrust upward.

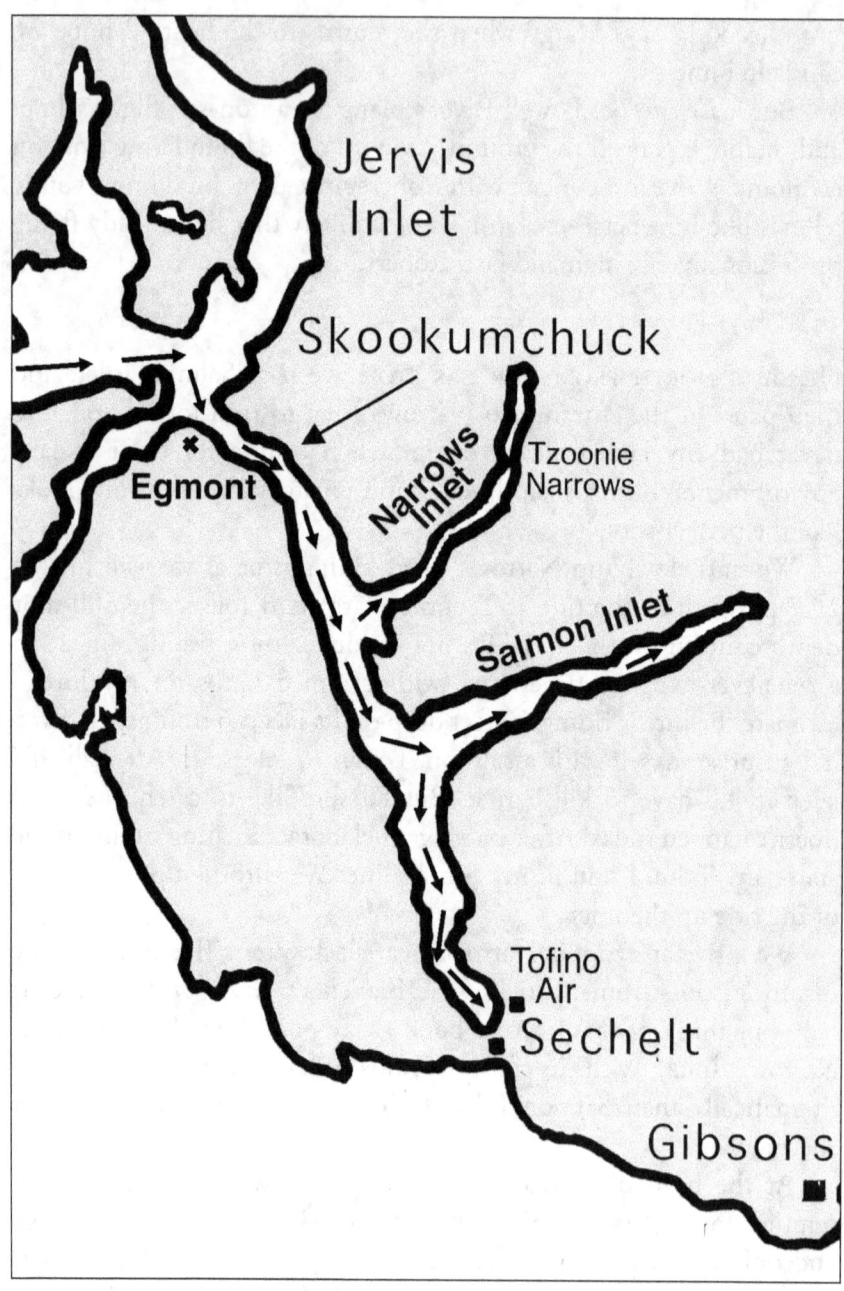

But evening outflow winds could be a problem. Fortunately, we'll be pushed from the north shore by these downslope winds, nudging us out of danger. Yet, I recall breaking anchor in the middle of the night

Head of Narrows Inlet

at Hotham Sound during the strong push of outflow winds, and this is a visual duplicate of that location. So I remain suspicious and attentive as we swing with the breeze.

It's a calm night, and the anchor holds fine. In the morning, Margy drives us out of the bay and back down the inlet. We arrive at Tzoonie Narrows a half-hour before slack water, but Margy feels comfortable piloting us through the significant swirls. This is good practice for her, and a turning point in her previous fears of rapids. She maneuvers the boat through the narrows nicely, barely slowing at the challenge of the current.

We exit Narrows Inlet and turn north towards Skookumchuck. We're early for the turn of the tide at the famous rapids, so we use the opportunity to troll the entrance. We slip along the west shore, with the Deep-6 and its attached flasher and lure trailing behind. Then we cross to a small island, and back to the west shore again. By now, the current is about to turn, so we continue toward Roland Point.

I begin to reel-in my line. But it's a tough retrieval, compounded by our forward motion and the current, and I seem to be dragging a chunk of seaweed, or is it a fish? As my lure approaches the surface, I feel a fish fighting. This is too small to be a big salmon, but it's a good-sized catch – a two-foot green spotted fish I don't readily identify. Then I realize it's a painted greenling. Ling cod, which frequent the chuck near Powell River, are a subspecies of the greenling. It's not a salmon, but a nice catch for me that I release back into the south entrance of Skookumchuck.

We have enough fuel to bypass Egmont and continue home. Rounding Scotch Fir Point, we're met by developing southeasterly winds in the Strait of Georgia. They provide a push for the last leg of our trip, but it's a bumpy ride in 3-foot swells. Ahead, I can see the distinct edge of the approaching cold front. It's a weather system that's been advertised for several days.

Dark clouds span the entire horizon to the north. This storm is not forecast to be a major weather-producer, but it's also not very summer-like. Then again, as every indicator has been telling us on this trip, summer is definitely over.

Chapter 3

Solo

Since my life experience rests more with aviation than nautical pursuits, I often compare my late-in-life introduction to boating with flying. Indeed, there are lots of similarities, and one of them is solo experience on the sea.

A pilot's initial solo flight is during his early training, and it's an exhilarating experience. To be free of your flight instructor and on your own is proof you've truly attained the primary skills of a pilot. In reality, you've been master of the aircraft for some time, since the instructor forces a new pilot to complete all the necessary tasks repeatedly and without assistance prior to the first solo. But suddenly realizing you're truly alone in the airplane is an eye-opening experience, and one not taken lightly.

Similarly, the first few times I set sail alone in *Halcyon Days* weren't particularly challenging from the standpoint of needing new skills. But there's a sense of accomplishment when alone in a boat that fosters the feeling of being a real "captain." Since most of my boating is with Margy (as is most of my flying), I've come to rely on her as my safety check. Without her aboard, I find myself more attentive and less complacent.

As much as I enjoy Margy's companionship on the water, our Bayliner is a small vessel for a voyage of any length. It's amazing how much bigger the boat seems when I'm at sea by myself.

Like flying, boating by myself provides another significant gift – a sense of confidence that carries over to nearly everything. Like most of the important experiences in life, solo activities build character.

Today, *Halcyon Days* is ready to go into the chuck for the first time this summer. I've determinedly declared my intent (again) to voyage farther north. I'm headed indirectly for Lund, where the boat will be moored for the summer months. Rather than going direct, I plan to travel on a solo voyage for a few days, eventually meeting Margy to secure the Bayliner in this new (to us) seasonal harbour.

John, Margy, and I (Bro, too!) work together at the airport to hook up the truck to the trailer, and at one point it takes all three (four!) of us. The Bayliner has been in the airport hangar for winter maintenance, and we'll now make the short tow to Westview Harbour. John connects the safety chains to the truck, while I hook up the wiring harness for the taillights, and Margy removes the trailer's wheel chocks. Bro supervises.

John then pulls the trailer forward, out of the hangared storage spot. He stops briefly, while Margy and Bro hop in the truck's passenger seat and I walk behind the trailer to check the lights. Before I get aboard the truck, there's one more thing to do before we leave.

"I'd better try backing up," John yells back to me.

The trailer's surge brake system is often fickle. The brakes themselves work fine, but the signal through the wiring harness sometimes falsely tells the brakes to engage when backing up. It's a bummer to get to the launch ramp, only to realize you can't back into the water. Such is the case today, except we catch it before we leave.

John hops out of the truck and pulls the wire connector out of the bumper socket to scrape off the contacts with his pocketknife. Usually, it's nothing more than a corroded connection. But today, we need to take it a step further.

"Margy, pump the brake pedal," says John.

With Brody plopped in the center seat, she needs to get out of the truck and walk around to the other side to get a straight shot at the brake pedal.

Meanwhile, I check the fuses, and John fiddles with the connector. Bro is out of the truck now, too, running around, checking every corner of the open-ended hangars for an elusive cat he saw here once, many years ago – he never gives up.

Finally, the surge brakes are working properly, although we're not sure what we've adjusted, and Margy backs up to test the fix. Of course, the problem with the repair is we don't really know how we've fixed it. Which is one of the many reasons I never launch a boat from a trailer without John. If this occurs again at the launch ramp, he'll figure it out.

We drive down Duncan Avenue to Westview Harbour, where John successfully backs the trailer into position at the ramp. It's a flawless launch, and within minutes the Bayliner is temporarily tied to the dock finger, ready to go. Since everything I need was loaded aboard the boat at the hangar, there's no reason to delay any further.

John and Margy wait while I climb up to the command bridge. It's another clumsy cold start for me, but then the motor purrs. As Margy unties the dock lines, I yell down to her, John, and Bro.

"Goin' to Alaska," I boast, which they know is far from the truth, but no one (not even me) knows where I'm going yet.

"Okay, have a good trip," replies John.

"No food though, but I've got some dog goodies for Bro. Can he go with me?"

I hold up a pouch of dog treats I've retrieved from my backpack for special effect.

John laughs and gives me his classic drawn-out "No…" that means "not in your lifetime."

I shift into reverse to pull the boat away from the dock, and then into forward to swing around the tight confines of the launch area. With no other boats present, I actually look like I know what I'm doing. And I'm off!

* * * * *

I CRUISE WEST OF SAVARY and then Hernando Island, towards Mitlenatch, while watching the GPS to stay well clear of Mystery and Grant's Reef. Then it's pretty much straight to Heriot Bay, which proves I really did have a destination in the back of my mind, at least to begin my trip. Not surprisingly, I'm going back (as I do again and again) to one of my favourite local spots, but maybe this time I'll continue beyond Quadra Island to the great inlets of the Broughtons. It's just a matter of adequate weather and time. My planned meeting with Margy at Lund could be delayed by a mere phone call.

My lack of freshly-packed food (there's always non-refrigerated stock aboard) dictates the route today. There's patio dining at Heriot

Bay Inn, and a good-sized store right up the road to buy the provisions I'll need for the rest of the trip. Add a gas dock, and it's the perfect place to start a trip north. To say it's one of my favourite destinations is to say the very least.

When navigating around the point at Rebecca Spit, I slow to no-wake speed. Although I'm focused on docking at what can be a busy location, I sneak a peak back to my left, into the anchorage at Drew Harbour, where Margy and I visited last year. Not a single boat is anchored here, which is no surprise. It's still early in the season (late May), and the deteriorating economy this year is probably big factor in the scarcity of boats I'll see on this trip.

At the gas dock, the fuel attendant is missing, but a call on the intercom outside the dock office brings an immediate response from the hotel lobby. The gas assistant is down the ramp quickly, so young looking that I forgo my normal inquiry about how business has been lately. It's likely his first year on the job, with little to compare to regarding the level of activity. Indirectly, however, he says it all when I ask if I can park long enough to eat at the inn.

"You can park anywhere. No one's coming today."

Of course, what he really means is no one has made a reservation for transient moorage today, but it does tell the whole story. The parking area is nearly empty. Then again, it's only May.

Mid-day dining on the outside deck is always enjoyable here. Today, only one other table is occupied. After lunch, when I stop at the hotel's gift shop, I notice that the three copies of *Up the Strait* on their shelf are not autographed, so I mention it to the clerk.

"These are mine," I say. "Would you like me to sign them?"

"Sure!" she says. "That's nice of you."

I smile, and open to the title page, where I scribble some remarks and sign my name. Then I open the second of the books while the clerk watches quietly.

"It's not really my book though," I state matter-of-factly.

The clerk looks startled, not quite sure what to say. Then I add: "Just kidding!" (Not everyone understands my sense of humour, including many of my readers.)

Up the road at the convenience store, I select a fresh-looking wrapped sandwich, a bottle of milk, and an apple pie. Along with the normal food stored in the Bayliner, I'll have plenty for tonight and tomorrow morning. My plan now is to spend at least one night in nearby Drew Harbour, with another chance tomorrow to restock what little food I need. Often, especially on solo voyages, I prefer to eat light (or not so light in cafes), rather than fire up the barbecue and prepare a full meal for one person. I consider it part of the fun of being alone.

Back at the dock, I take the opportunity (with no marina parking rush) to refill my freshwater tank. Then I spend some leisurely time on the command bridge installing a new chart software chip in the GPS and playing with the sonar settings. As the first day on the chuck for the season, it's fun to get things going again, and doing so without being rushed is a good feeling.

When I leave Heriot Bay, the trip is mighty short. I take the first right turn past the ferry terminal, and pull into Drew Harbour. Since the bay is empty, I pick a spot halfway down the beach in 30 feet of water. The tides are moderate here, and there's no significant current, with good holding conditions in a mud bottom.

Once anchored, I sit on the aft deck, watching the sunset and making a list of new-season projects regarding the boat, such as a new carpet for the center aisle (only 2-foot by 10-foot), a fuel consumption test, and replacement of interior light covers. One of the items on my list is the toilet water system, which doesn't seem to be refilling properly. I grab a bucket, fill it with water from the sink, and pour it into the head. Pumping the handle, after a slight delay, brings water into the bowl. The pump feels normal after this simple priming, so I cross the item off my list.

I make a separate list for my visit to Campbell River's Canadian SuperStore tomorrow. By now, I'm pretty focused on a visit to Campbell River, and then spending a second night near there before meeting Margy at Lund the following day. Or maybe I'll actually go farther north towards the Broughtons, and delay my plans for Lund. A loose schedule on the chuck suits me just fine.

* * * * *

THE NEXT MORNING, I travel around the south side of Quadra Island, and into the tidal flow that usually dominates an approach to Campbell River. Today, the GPS shows a speed reduction of 4 knots at cruise, verifying a flooding tide from the north.

I push into the current, and feel the Bayliner deviating from its heading, hunting left and right. I recognize my status as an amateur boater when a 4-knot current prevents me from tracking straight ahead at cruise, but it's another gentle introduction to what lies ahead this year. Starting under controlled conditions always feels comfortable.

At the Campbell River gas dock, I find fewer boats than normal. When I pull in towards the pumps, I sit on the command bridge looking down at the awaiting fuel attendant. He's bobbing around in my field of view, as the Bayliner struggles through the not-so-gentle wake from a slow but big departing tug.

"Watch out! Here comes an amateur," I announce.

That admission always gets a smile of respect from gas docks all over BC. Even when I make a sloppy arrival, after proclaiming my layman status, the reception is routinely friendly.

I've docked here several times previously, but the arrangement looks different. Somehow the gas pumps seem to now reside on a smaller dock, or maybe I previously used the commercial boat area nearer the office.

"How long has this dock been here?" I ask, after hopping out of the boat.

"About 20 years," replies the attendant.

"Oh."

For my trip to the shopping centre, the attendant suggests I tie up a short distance from the gas pumps on a side finger. Off-season boating has a lot to say for itself.

Lunch at the fish and chips restaurant hits the spot. Then I make a few purchases at the SuperStore, including the carpet I need for the Bayliner, a variety of small batteries for electronic devices, and the luxury of a new portable AM-FM radio.

Back at the boat, I rig up a fishing pole for jigging, which indirectly tells me I've finally decided on my cruising direction. Sentry Shoal (to the south) isn't far away, and I've never fished there. Someday I'm going to catch my second salmon. It's been seven years since my first. Partly it's my lack of seriousness about fishing, since I get too much enjoyment at just making a few leisurely casts and calling it a day. I spend more time rigging up than fishing.

Leaving the fuel dock, I maneuver through the marina entrance, and turn right towards Sentry Shoal – so now I know where I'm going, headed back towards the south and Lund. Part of my enjoyment on the chuck is determining destinations on-the-fly. It may sound indecisive (and it is), but it's enjoyable that way. Every kilometre is a surprise, even to the captain.

At Sentry Shoal, I have typical luck (meaning lack of it), but I retain my normal satisfaction of having the freedom to fish almost anywhere in this big ocean. It seems like an amazing privilege, luck or no luck.

Since Mitlenatch Island is so near, and the tide is high, I decide to investigate the small bay on the east side. I've seen boats anchored there, but the bay is tight. Maybe today I can slip in at high water as the only occupant. The other bay on the island is wide and open, but not well protected for an overnight stay.

Mitlenatch's Bird Island

When I pull in past Bird Island, gulls are perched everywhere. Their shrill voices raise a cacophony that would be difficult to sleep through. Maybe they will sleep quietly, but if I anchor near here, it will be several hours before they calm down.

A little farther in towards the bay opening, I find sea lions sitting on the rocks all along the shore, barking up a storm. Noisy birds to the right, even louder sea lions to the left. Some of these big mammals are larger than my dinghy, *Mr. Bathtub*, and certainly a lot heavier. These are amazing animals, and I'm thrilled to be so close to them, but there'll be no peace for anyone who anchors here. So before I even enter the cove, I'm outta' there.

My alternate thought for an overnight anchorage in the direction of Lund is the Copeland Islands, though there's something about anchoring so close to home that makes me feel like I'm acting too restrained. Nevertheless, I navigate around the north end of the islands and enter Thulin Passage, heading south. The main anchorage near the marine park sign holds only one large sailboat today, but swinging space is limited for a second craft. Plus, it would seem impolite to anchor near someone else when most of the Strait of Georgia is empty

Mitlenatch sea lions

of boats. So I idle my way down the shore towards the end of the island that protects the entrance to the marine park. I drop my anchor in a spot that lies at the end of the small island, where the narrow waterway to the other side of the Copelands begins. This location has lots of late afternoon sun, since the channel to the west is wide and angled towards the northwest. In fact, sunset here is spectacular.

Copeland Islands sunset

* * * * *

THE NEXT MORNING, I linger on the aft deck, reading and listening to the radio. The ride from here to Lund will take only 15 minutes.

As my scheduled meeting time with Margy at 10 o'clock approaches, I raise anchor and cruise the short distance to Lund. When I pull into the fuel dock, Margy is there to meet me.

"Fran says you can pull around the corner into the harbour and call her on the radio. She plans to park you near the pump-out station, wherever that is."

Fran seems like an old friend, although I've never met her. Margy has been coordinating our anticipated mooring here for weeks, and it sounds like all will work out well. The harbour is tight, and we know we'll be rafted up to other boats, but we're prepared for it, although this is our first experience with rafted moorage.

"Can you call her on the phone when I enter the harbour, so I don't have to use the radio?" I ask.

As comfortable as I am with air traffic control communication in my Piper Arrow, I seldom use the VHF in the Bayliner. There's little difference in air and sea communication procedures, and I have decades of comfortable skill with air traffic control towers, but almost none with marinas. To make matters worse, the radio on the command bridge is wedged low and almost out of sight. Just setting the frequency and volume is a difficult process from the driver's seat. As a result, I seldom use the VHF.

"I'll try to phone her," says Margy. "But Fran says they depend on the radio around here."

Fortunately, when I come around the corner, Fran is on the end of the dock, motioning for me to swing around the next finger. By the time I maneuver around the corner, Fran and Margy are on a large sailboat, which is rafted up to a small trawler, ready to receive my lines as the third vessel in line. This will be *Halcyon Days*' home port for the next three months.

Rafting at Lund Harbour

* * * * *

BACK-TO-BACK SOLO TRIPS on the chuck are uncommon for me, but five days later, I launch from Lund, again by myself. Margy drops me off, but she's headed for Bellingham tomorrow, and I decide to spend the time at sea. In fact, if all goes well, I'd like to go farther north than ever before. The weather forecast is good, and I've got the time. So off I go.

But first I face the rafting dilemma. The Bayliner is still parked near the pump-out station at the same dock location, but now I'm third in a four-boat raft. As soon as I clamber over two boats to get aboard *Halcyon Days*, Fran shows up. It seems like she's been idly waiting for five days for me to return so she can help me get out of the harbour.

"Here, I'll give you a hand," she says, stepping through the Bayliner's aft deck, on her way to the last boat on the outside.

She unties the lines connecting *Halcyon Days* to the outer boat, sweeps the fenders aside, and quickly pushes the 30-foot aluminum crew boat out of the way. I'm not sure where she's going with it, or how, but my departure route is immediately open. She waves as she steps onto another rafted boat directly in front of mine, briskly slings fenders over the side, and ties the crew boat's lines. Then she's gone.

I finish loading the Bayliner, ducking below sails and maneuvering across the two boats that separate me from the dock. I take a few minutes to review the charts to the north and scan through a magazine article entitled "Where's Gas?" Refuel facilities to the north are limited, so I want to plan my stops accordingly. A few minutes later, just before 2 o'clock, I'm on my way.

First stop will be Refuge Cove, a good place to refuel, since it sets me up for a stretch that may take me as far as another fuel stop at Blind Channel, an entry point to the Broughton Archipelago. Big Bay, about halfway between Refuge Cove and Blind Channel, no longer has fuel, as "Where's Gas?" has informed me.

My stop at Refuge Cove takes a little longer than planned, which may interfere with any prospects I have for making slack tide at Yuculta Rapids. The delay is my own fault, as I take time to explore around a small float house that's tied up near the gas dock. It's actually a barge with a house on it, bordered by lots of hanging plants. This large segment of dock space will need to be cleared before the summer traffic arrives, considering how crowded this cove will become in another month.

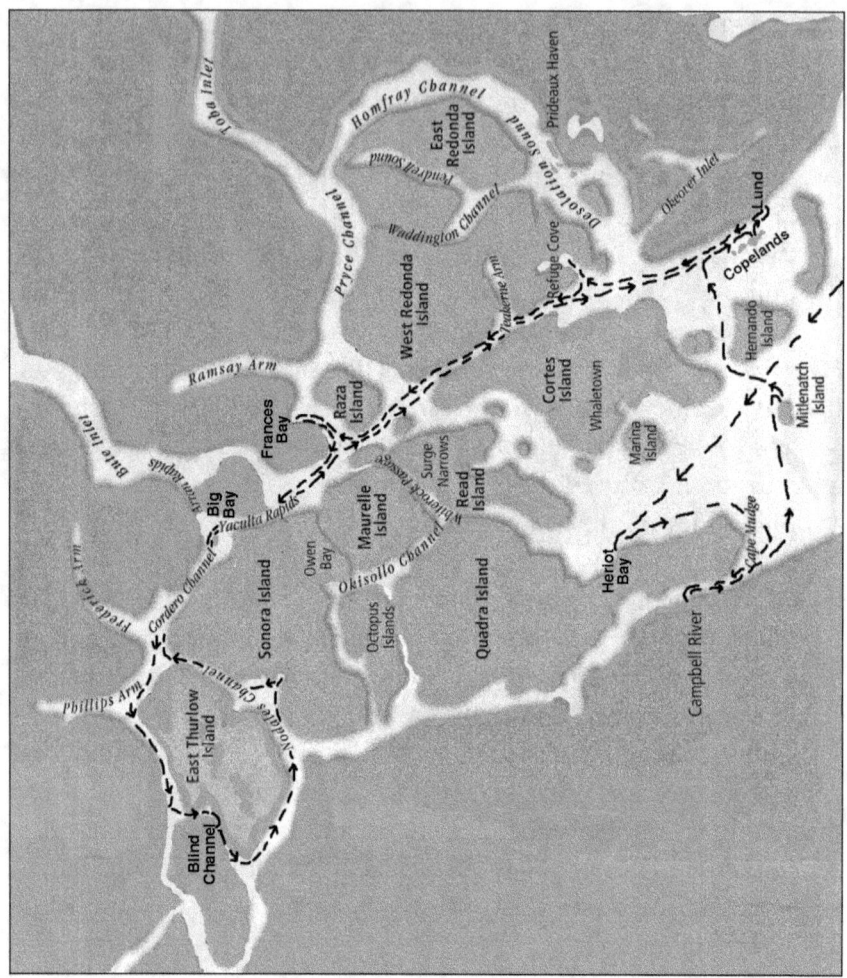

It takes two trips to the store to get my gas – one to ask instructions ("Just pump the gas yourself, and bring back the litre reading"), and one to pay my bill. This isn't a big delay, and there's no sense hurrying. Racing the tides seldom works. There's always an alternate plan that will work fine.

Leaving Refuge Cove, and progressing farther north, it becomes obvious I won't make it through the Yuculta Rapids today, so I stop short and anchor at Frances Bay on Ramsay Arm. In 50-feet of water, I drop anchor on a flat shelf that eventually slopes into deep water. The wind is nearly calm, and the bay should be sheltered tonight from the prevailing wind, which is expected to be light. So I feel comfortable with the location and enjoy the evening.

Floating barge at Refuge Cove

Just before sunset, a sailboat arrives and positions itself in stern-tie position at the head of the bay, a comfortable distance away. The wind goes dead calm, and I sleep well.

Frances Bay

* * * * *

I SET MY ALARM WRONG, and awake the next morning at 7:30, later than planned. The tide will turn at Yuculta at 7:58, so I'll never make it in time. As always, there's an alternate plan, and today it involves enjoying the morning in Frances Bay, and then leaving at noon to fish for salmon along the way.

The next slack tide will be turning to flood, which equates to a flow to the south. My cruising guides indicates a turn to ebb is the best way to go through Yuculta Rapids from the south, since slower sailboats can keep pace with the tide as the ebb proceeds northward. Shortly beyond this first round of rapids is another fast flow farther north near Little Dent Island, and slack tide this afternoon will occur there first. In other words, today I'll literally be going against the tide, and it will be impossible to catch up. Although I missed the more-favourable turn to ebb by getting up late today, I should be fine with my faster boat. Still, it would be best to start through a little early to provide a pad against the tide near Little Dent.

Thirty minutes before the turn of the tide, I start into the rapids, which are now easily navigable. I pass the luxurious lodge on the left, with its spacious but empty lines of docks. Big Bay is to the right, looking like an interesting future destination. Turning towards the exit at Little Dent Island, I enter Gillard Passage, where I slow to nearly idle as I pass a sportfishing boat. Slack tide is an ideal time for salmon, and it would be shame to miss the opportunity. But I don't want to be caught in high current near Little Dent Island, so I come back up onto plane after passing the fishing boat, and keep going, although the water here isn't even a bit turbulent.

When I reach Little Dent Island, I know I'm nearly out of this region of rapids. The flow here is significant, flooding back towards Big Bay, but it's an easy escape from here to the calmer water to the north. So I take some time to try again for my second salmon of the decade. I rig up with a heavy jigging lure, and toss it overboard. My lure is dragged to the bottom almost immediately, a victim of the swirling current. This seems like the perfect spot for salmon.

Bam! It's a big fish! Or is it a big rock? When I try to retrieve my line, there's no movement on the other end of the line, but a lot of resistance. There's no doubt I've hooked the bottom, probably wound viciously around the rocks by the spiraling water below. There's no solution except to back over the lure, and try to yank it from its rocky prison. It's no surprise when this tactic doesn't work here. I retrieve my line with the lure missing.

But I don't give up. I tie on another swivel and attach a new lure. This time, I pull out of the swift flow, which is getting stronger by the minute, and angle over towards the shore just above the beginning of the rapids. The salmon environment here looks even better, but 15 minutes in this fine-looking spot produces no results. At least I don't lose another lure.

But I do mess up my prop. Fortunately, it's entirely temporary, as my fishing line swirls in the near-rapids, and twists itself around the propeller. To get at the problem, I pull into an area of calm water near shore, untie *Mr. Bathtub,* and push it to the side of the boat so I can get at the transom. With the dinghy riding safely on the starboard side, I raise the stern-drive's leg. From the swim grid, I'm able to unwind the fishing line from the prop, even retrieving my lure.

The route from here to Blind Channel is particularly picturesque, with high mountains dropping into the sea on both sides. The current flow I expect during the approach to Blind Channel (per my cruising guidebook) seems within the Bayliner's capabilities, even at maximum flow, but I'm not sure this is the case. So, with time to spare, I decide to drop anchor to wait until maximum current passes. I look at several possible spots for a day hook, but the shoreline just before the turn into Blind Channel is too populated to suit me. I find a nondescript beach near Green Point, anchoring briefly there, listening to the radio and catnapping in the V-berth.

By the time I enter Blind Channel, the flow is so reduced that it seems unnoticeable, indicating that the channel could probably be easily navigated in the Bayliner at maximum current. Still, it was worth the wait to increase my comfort level.

When I pull into the Blind Channel Marina, I'm surprised to find no boats in the spacious docks, and nobody at the gas dock. I've seen photos of this resort, and they all contain lots of boats and lots of people. But not today.

I walk up to the store to find someone to pump gas. The restaurant is closed, but a cold soda from the store certainly hits the spot. There are really no provisions I need, so after refueling, I'm on my way again.

Headed down the channel towards Johnstone Strait, the wind begins to raise waves that are near my personal limit. The good news:

these are fair-weather winds from the northwest. The bad news: the gusts are strong. I'm now the farthest north I've ever been in a boat, and the temptation is to turn north in the strait and enter the Broughton Archipelago, but that would be into the wind. Besides, it's time to think about turning towards home. So I make the decision (again on-the-fly) to head south.

I enter Johnstone Strait to find significant whitecaps and a large container ship heading up the strait. I turn south, maneuver out of the way of the big ship, and am immediately impressed by the immensity of the strait. But if I can make it only a few kilometres, I should be protected from the strong wind as I turn towards Thurston Bay.

On the command bridge, I'm sprayed now and then as the bow comes down into four-foot waves in this following sea. But then the conditions seem to improve a bit, and I settle into a fairly comfortable ride, knowing the turn to Thurston isn't far ahead.

As expected, when I make the turn, conditions improve rapidly, now in the shadow of the northwest wind. In Thurston Bay, I find a small cove that seems safe for the night. The wind is blocked here, although a few gusts push the Bayliner towards shore as the boat swings on anchor. The best feature of this location is that it's very private, with no other boats in sight.

After sunset, conditions change suddenly, and the breeze grows into a howling wind. Maybe it's the drop in temperature that sets things off, but the change comes at a time when there's not enough daylight to move to another anchorage. So I spend a good portion of the night checking my position against the cliffs, to make sure I'm not dragging anchor. When I listen to the marine weather report, nearby Chatham Point in Johnstone Strait reports a consistent blow of 40 knots from the northwest. The wind is half that here, but still enough to keep me awake and nervous. Now the privacy of this spot has changed into a feeling of uncomfortable remoteness.

At about 5 am, the wind reduces to a mere breeze, although Chatham Point is still reporting 30 knots with a wind warning for the rest of the day. So, when I raise anchor, I head north and away from Johnstone Strait, which will allow me to rejoin the main channel and track back the same way I came the previous day. This route turns out to be nearly calm.

I navigate past Little Dent Island, where I contribute another lure to the deep rocks. Within seconds of tossing it into the water, zip! – it's gone.

Then I continue through Gillard Passage during slack tide, past Big Bay, and out the Yuculta Rapids. I retrace my path through Lewis Channel, traveling along the east side of Cortes Island. I bypass Refuge Cove and head nonstop to Lund.

This time I enter Lund Harbour as if I know what I'm doing. I contact Fran on the VHF radio to arrange parking, and she directs me back to the spot near the pump-out station.

"Just raft up on the outside, and give me a call if you need help."

No problem. I'm used to rafting the Bayliner in and out of position now. Of course, solo cruising provides direct benefits when it comes to almost any situation such as this one – a sense of confidence that carries over to nearly everything.

Chapter 4

The Imperfect Boat

When I believe in something, little snags won't change my perspective. Even obvious obstacles may not change my mind.

When it comes to my perfect boat, it would take a lot to distract me. However, during one of the longest stretches of ideal summer weather in recent British Columbia history, *Halcyon Days* was able to challenge my perspective.

That year, when I began making plans to visit the Broughtons (again), I became concerned with starting and idle problems with the Bayliner. The boat had been in the water for only a month, with two May trips under my belt. On both overnighters, the engine started poorly and refused to idle smoothly enough to allow comfortable shifting into gear. Both problems were enigmas, since the difficulties seemed duplications of the problems prior to the engine replacement the previous year. Since this was a completely different engine, why would the starting and idling quandaries be so similar?

John and I spend an afternoon troubleshooting the ignition system, since it seems a prime culprit. The starter cranks fine, but the engine refuses to fire until its good and ready, and then runs rough at the lowest throttle setting. At normal speeds, the engine operates fine.

We thoroughly check the spark plugs, ignition leads, and points. Everything is within standards. The carburetor is the next suspect, and I'm certain we're now homing in on the problem. But even an overhaul of the carburetor doesn't solve the problem. One day when John is working on the boat, chasing every last possibility, he's diverted in another direction – low compression.

Sure, the boat seems to have increasing difficulty coming up on plane, but the hull is getting covered with critters more and more each day, the nemesis of boats sitting in salt water. However, the buildup of marine growth on the hull doesn't seem enough to equate to this deterioration in performance. On the other hand, what does this have to do with poor starts and rough idle, since the engine runs smooth in cruise? Deteriorating compression is a sign of old age, and this engine is nearly new. On the other hand, a trip as far as the Broughtons would be dangerous with the threat of unreliable starts and possible flameout when shifting gears.

"I'm not surprised the engine has lost some of its compression, although it's strange for such a new engine," I tell John. "But I'm not convinced it's the source of the starting and idle problems."

"Well, we've checked everything else," he replies. "I've asked the boat shop to make a differential compression check, which is better than my direct check, and it should identify the source of the pressure loss."

"Okay, but before we get the shop involved, let's take one more look at the carburetor."

"We've already tweaked it to death," says John. "Even overhauled it."

What did this new engine have in common with the old engine? It suddenly comes to me!

"What about the air filter?" I ask. "We used the old filter on the new engine. Don't you remember? The new filter was all dented, so we used the old one."

"But that isn't it," he replies. "I've checked the filter, and it's fine."

"But the old engine was a Chevy 305. The new one is a 350. Wouldn't a bigger engine need more air?"

I've got it! I just know this is the problem, and it explains everything. But John isn't buying it.

"Both engines use the same filter," he says. "Besides, we've bypassed the filter, by removing it. We've done that, you know."

He's right, of course. But I make him go through the process of swapping out the filter anyway. The problem isn't solved. But before we go to the expense of a minor overhaul, I still suspect the carburetor. So I ask John to install a new one – again.

"Ridiculous, " says John. "A waste of money."

"I know, but will you replace it for me anyway?"

"Let's see what the shop says about the compression first," says John.

We wait for the shop's verdict, and it isn't a good one, nor is it conclusive.

"The low compression seems to be from bad valves," says John. "That means it'll need to go to the shop."

I'm not going to change John's opinion on this or any other matter once he's made up his mind. But he gives in to my request to try (another) carburetor first. Now we have a different carburetor and the same problem. The cost of this project is climbing exponentially, and we haven't made any progress. Finally, I give in – the boat is scheduled to go to the shop for new valves.

But try to get a recreational boat into a British Columbia marine shop in the heart of summer. I may be a local customer, but commercial boats get a priority. The Bayliner sits awaiting work. And it sits for a full month.

Finally, with the new valves installed, John conducts the sea trials. The results are inconclusive.

"Starts fine now," he reports. "And idles good, too. Doesn't stall when you shift. But I'm not sure about the power."

What John has found is one of those things that's difficult to wrap your arms around. He knows the boat well, and he perceives it's slow getting up onto plane. With new valves, it should have increased compression, but his perception is the boat has less cruise power than before the overhaul. And he's also concerned with the engine temperature, which seems to be running a little higher than prior to the repairs.

"When I started towards Harwood Island, all seemed fine," he says. "But then I stopped and turned around. It just didn't seem to want to get up on plane for the trip back to the harbour."

Waves and wind are factors here, of course. Which makes a sea trial even more nebulous.

"Try it, and see what you think?" he says.

"Okay. I'll check the GPS speed, too," I suggest. "I can compare that to the performance before we went into the shop. And I'll keep my eye on the temperature."

My sea trial runs are inconclusive. The boat starts okay, and gets up on plane, but I'm not sure if the performance during cruise is improved. In theory, I should have a better feel for this boat's performance than John. But when John questions something, it makes you wonder.

* * * * *

DURING THIS GORGEOUS SUMMER, the region's longest period of fair weather in over a decade, the Bayliner isn't the only boat experiencing unusual problems. The Campion, used for transportation to and from my cabin on the lake, has developed a stern-drive rumbling that indicates a U-joint or bearing requiring attention. As I describe it to John, the rumble of "marbles" in the engine compartment seems to be getting progressively worse.

"I don't feel comfortable driving it any more than necessary," I report. "For now, I'll use the tin boat when I come to town, until we can get the Campion fixed."

Easier said than done. The tin boat is a joy to drive, and it's totally adequate for trips to town under favorable wind conditions. But the small boat isn't capable of making the trip when significant waves develop. Even the up-lake winds of fair summer days can pound the hull beyond its practical limit. So I time my trips around the weather.

"Margy and I are leaving the Shinglemill in the tin boat now," I say to John over the cell phone. "Nice evening. Almost calm."

"How soon can you bring the Campion down the lake, so we can pull it out and work on it?" he asks.

"Maybe tomorrow, if the weather permits," I reply. "Margy can drive the Campion down the lake, and I'll bring the tin boat. Then I'll just use the tin boat until we get the marbles fixed."

There's more for us to talk about, but I'm trying to talk on the phone while driving the tin boat as we navigate out of the Shinglemill breakwater. I motion to Margy to swap seats with me. I shift into neutral and move forward, while she moves to the stern to operate the 15-horsepower outboard.

Although Margy doesn't hesitate to exchange positions, I notice she looks over the idling Honda closely before she shifts into gear. Then I realize she's driven this boat and motor combination only once before.

Until we replaced our old outboard motor, she operated that engine regularly. Although both outboards were rated at 15 horsepower, this new four-stroke has a lot more muscle than the worn out Evinrude. And our tin boat can be slippery.

She accelerates slowly, getting a feel for the engine, finally reaching a slow cruise that seems to suit her. Meanwhile, I continue to discuss boats, quads, and cabin projects with John over the cell phone. The new motor is so quiet it's easy to talk on the phone during slow cruise, until Margy goes into a sudden turn to the left, then a turn back to the right. The boat starts to oscillate laterally at a rate that both surprises and frightens me.

"Whoa!" I yell, yanking the phone from my ear. "Cut the throttle!"

Margy fumbles for a moment, we continue to oscillate, and I'm not willing to wait any longer.

"Hit the kill switch!" I yell.

She does, and everything is back under control almost immediately. The tin boat drifts to a stop while straightening itself quickly. The crisis is over.

"What was that?" says John, when I finally get back to the phone.

"Oh, that was just Margy," I say. "She was practicing her Immelmann turns?"

"Her what?"

"It's a scary flying maneuver. You should have seen it."

I feel terrible. My normal way of handling Margy's training in boats has fallen apart in an instant. While distracted by my phone call to John, I've asked her to take command of a motor she's never operated. Of course, I should have trained her in this boat-motor combination previously, but I didn't. Now I've put her in a situation that's over her head. This tin boat can get away from you in an instant, if you're not ready for its tricky cruise conditions. It was entirely my fault, and I know it.

But Margy doesn't relinquish her seat in the stern, although I expect it. After I hang up the telephone, we sit bobbing in the water, discussing the need to make small heading corrections in this boat at cruise, and what to do if oscillations occur. Then she pulls on the starter rope, and the motor fires on the first pull. Margy shifts into gear and accelerates slowly. Pretty soon, she's at nearly full throttle and looking comfortable. At this high speed, her hat flies back on her head, caught on her pony-tail, so she pulls off her cap. Then she settles into a comfortable command mode for the 30-minute trip back to Hole in the Wall.

Margy drives the tin boat

* * * * *

THE NEXT DAY, MARGY DRIVES THE CAMPION to the Shinglemill, while I follow her in the tin boat. We'll park the Campion in its normal berth until John can retrieve it, leaving the smaller boat at the transient dock for lake operations until the repairs are complete. One boat (the Campion) will be on its trailer at the airport, while another (the Bayliner) awaits consensus as to whether it's ready to travel on the chuck again.

We drive the truck directly to the airport, where Margy will catch a Pacific Coastal flight to Vancouver, and then the bus to Bellingham to visit her mother. After dropping her off, I head for Westview Harbour to combine another engine test with an overnighter on the chuck. I've promised John I won't go far, in case the engine doesn't work out as expected. But I hate to waste the chance for a night on the boat. Van Anda seems the perfect destination – close enough for John to put a toolbox in his truck and take a short ferry ride to Texada Island.

The engine start goes good, and it goes bad. It's good in the sense that the motor starts immediately after two shots of throttle, just like the good ol' days. But bad because of what happens next. The engine starts to run rough at idle and decays in RPM. I try to slide the throttle forward to catch it before the motor dies, but the engine flames out. Not the best start for my perfect boat, recently returned from the shop with a new set of valves.

The restart is rough, and the engine dies almost immediately. Am I facing a flooded condition? I try a normal start with the throttle barely cracked. When that doesn't work, I go for a flooded start (throttle full forward), and that eventually results in a rambling start. But it isn't a smooth beginning for my overnight trip.

Once the engine smoothes out and idles normally, I'm able to shift into gear without any problems. Thus, one of the difficulties (starting) is still in question. But another problem (shifting gears) seems to be totally solved.

When I throttle up outside the harbour, I let out a "Yahoo!" The acceleration is impressive, even though I'm headed into the waves, and I'm quickly on-plane at a fully-acceptable GPS speed of 23 knots. Then I throttle back enough to hear the slightly lower RPM I seek during cruise. The third problem (on-plane power) is solved for now, although I remember John's comments regarding how the performance seemed to deteriorate later in his engine test.

As soon as I'm on my way towards Texada Island, the waves grow quickly. A southeasterly wind is moving into the area, and whitecaps are moving up Malaspina Strait. Under these conditions, a short trip to Texada can be a challenge. My speed drops off rapidly, and now I seem to be falling off plane. Then again, it also seems the throttle has slipped back. If I had a normal tachometer, I'd be able to clearly tell, but my tach is in its typically fickle mood. Today, the tachometer reads off-scale high, providing meaningless information. Still, my ears say the rpm is lower, and the physical position of the throttle seems slightly reduced. So I power-up, and get back solidly on-plane again. Is this what John experienced? If so, my similar situation may be the result of increased wave heights coupled with a throttle that's slipped aft.

In a few minutes, I'm so occupied with the rough conditions in the strait that I have no time to test the power conditions. Looking towards Texada, I notice sizable waves crashing against the shore. This will be a short trip, and I should be able to handle such a challenge at slow speed. In fact, I've consciously slowed to 15 knots, and I've swung from a southerly heading (which would take me direct to Van Anda) to a more westerly course. That puts the waves behind me at a quartering angle that feels more comfortable, and points my bow at Blubber Bay. My new plan is to get across the strait with a following sea, and then follow the coast to Van Anda. Normally, I would expect the northern tip of Texada to be in the wind-shadow under these conditions, although visible whitecaps along the shoreline contradict that assumption. In any case, my current desire is to simply get out of the middle of Malaspina Strait.

As I get closer to Blubber Bay, the waves here are significant, so I turn back into the wind for a more direct route to Van Anda. I try slowing to 5 knots, but the wave fetch is slightly longer than my boat, causing the Bayliner to slap down hard between waves. Eight knots seems to work better, and that's where I stabilize.

As usual, I'm driving from the command bridge. Water is splashing up from the bow, drenching my shirt, face, and sunglasses. I take my glasses off, and button the neck of my shirt. In the cabin down below, I hear heavy items falling off the table or seat cushions, smashing to the floor. I hope my laptop computer isn't one of them.

Approaching Van Anda, conditions marginally improve, though still rough with plenty of whitecaps. Ahead of me, maneuvering outside the harbour entrance is a big sailboat. The vessel swings back and forth in front of *Halcyon Days*, sometimes tacking towards the harbour, sometimes leaning at an exciting angle. Why would anyone be sailing in these conditions? Of course, this question is being asked by someone who knows little about sailboats. I surmise the crew is having their own kind of fun, testing their individual limits on purpose. One thing for sure, the big sailboat, *Whisky Jack*, is periodically leaning in America's Cup fashion.

Farther south, another large sailboat seems angled towards the harbour, similarly under full sail. Maybe these two boats are traveling together, having their own rough-water race along the way.

I beat *Whisky Jack* to the entrance, pulling into the protected bay in nearly calm conditions. Behind me, furling its huge sails, the big sailboat gets ready to dock under the power of its small engine.

The outermost dock straight ahead is clearly labeled *Visitors*, and it's nearly empty. I plan to moor at the outer end, which looks like the best position for privacy. But as I head for my selected position, I notice a man walking towards the *Visitors* sign at a fast pace. He's obviously here to meet me. As I ease towards the dock, the fellow points towards the innermost section of the dock finger, and yells up to me on the command bridge.

"Pull around that boat! Come in behind the tent, where it's nice and protected."

"When the wharfinger meets my boat, I know one of two things," I shout over to him. "Either I'm in big trouble, or I'm getting some mighty personal treatment."

"You'll find out later, when my wife comes down to collect some money from you."

I pull behind the other two boats on the outer finger, both large sailboats. Then I swing towards the white tent, which is a visiting boaters area, including several green picnic tables. As I angle into the dock, bodies hop from the adjacent sailboat and from under the tent, ready to assist with lines. As they grab my ropes and begin to tie them, I shut the engine off, looking down at my volunteer dockhands.

"It takes five people to tie up my little boat," I remark. "And I bet it takes only two of you to sail that big one."

One of the women laughs: "Not really. We had five of us working to keep our boat going today."

While I'm being secured, *Whisky Jack*, under the instructions of the wharfinger, pulls into the outer spot where I was originally headed. A few minutes later, another 36-foot sailboat pulls into the only other available parking spot behind me. The visitor's dock has gone from nearly empty to full in a matter of 10 minutes. All big sailboats, except for me.

Bayliner at Van Anda

* * * * *

When I check things out below, I find my laptop is still secure in its case on the table. But a lot of water has been splashed around inside the cabin, the result of two open windows during my rough crossing of the strait. Live and learn.

My original plan to walk up to the Texada Inn for dinner is changed when I realize I still haven't eaten my lunch. Inside my cloth coolerbag is a big roast beef sandwich, some cookies, and a cold bottle of water. I'd planned to be on the chuck longer today, fishing off Texada. But when the conditions got rough, I headed straight for port. Now I'm ready for the sandwich, and it'll be plenty as my evening meal.

I spend the rest of the afternoon lounging on the Bayliner's aft deck, reading and enjoying the sun. Although the crossing was rough, there's still lingering warmth here and no sign of rain. The forecast is for moderating conditions tonight, followed by a full-fledged late summer storm tomorrow evening. Today's southeast winds were just a precursor. The morning should be fine for another day on the chuck, but I probably won't be able to eke out a second night.

When the wharfinger's wife arrives (or maybe she's the true wharfinger), I pay my $14 bill cheerfully. It's a small price to pay for such a nice moorage, with no shore power needed. No electricity, no shore water, no trash disposal – just me and my 24-foot Bayliner. The protected spot behind the tent pays for itself. I bob comfortably when an evening breeze comes up, rattling the tackle on the sailboats.

That night I call John to report my test results. I tell him I'll be able to accumulate more data tomorrow, since my on-plane test was so limited today. I also explain the Campion is now in its berth at the Shinglemill, waiting in line for its trip to the boat doctor – John, that is. This time, my physician will be working on the Campion on its trailer in the airport hangar.

"Let me know when you're ready to pull the Campion out of the water, so I can give you a hand," I suggest.

"Okay," he replies. "Guess it isn't a big priority now that you've moved to your tin boat."

"It'll work fine for me. I'll just limit my travel on the lake to weather good enough for a tin boat."

Plus, it's another excuse to drive the small aluminum boat. There are big boats, and there are little boats, but little boats can sometimes be the most fun of all.

* * * * *

I AWAKEN EARLY THE NEXT MORNING to find clear skies and no wind. For the perfect sea trial, I want to get going before waves develop. It takes only a few minutes to secure the cabin, shift battery power back to *Both*, and climb up to the command bridge. This will be a good test of a cold start. But if it doesn't work, I'll wake up the entire dock community with my engine's continued cranking, coughing, and spitting.

The results are the same as yesterday – a perfect start, followed by power decay, and than another attempt after pumping the throttle. And another, until finally, using flooded start procedures (throttle full forward), I get the engine running smoothly, but only after a momentary blast at high power.

I look around and see a light go on behind me, and a head pop out of an aft door across the dock.

"Can I give you a hand?" asks the man who is now on his aft deck. "I'll get your lines."

"No, I'm fine," I say, as I scramble down from the bridge to tend to my dock ropes. "Hope I didn't wake you up."

"No, no. I was already awake."

What about the rest of the boats?

I sneak out of the moorage as quietly as possible, the Bayliner shifting flawlessly without dying. If the starting problem is the only complication, John can probably adjust the choke. Since I've needed a flooded start twice during cold conditions, maybe it's an easy adjustment. That might also explain John's perceived problems when he was on-plane. But it wouldn't explain the possible overheat indications he identified.

When I exit the harbour, I go to full power, and *Halcyon Days* leaps up onto plane in the smooth sea. The GPS reads 25 knots, and holds at 22 when I throttle back. The tachometer is still off-scale high, completely worthless, but the rpm sounds like normal cruise. The temperature rises from 180 at idle to 195, where it stops. Although John feels that's a bit high, I'm comfortable with it. And now I'll be able to complete another test John has requested: "Come back to idle after a cruise run," he said the previous day. "Then open the engine compartment with the motor running. Try touching the exhaust risers to see if you can keep your hand on them. If not, it's running too hot."

Not only can I touch the risers, I can press my fingers against them without needing to pull them away due to the heat. I repeat this test several times, always with favourable results. And the temperature indication never rises above 195 on either the command bridge or the lower helm indicators.

Best of all, I don't experience the coming-off-plane problem John experienced. Except for yesterday, in those rough seas, the boat seems to have no power problems. Since sea conditions can be so changeable, it's not unexpected to get an occasional weirdness in this regard, something I've experienced even before the recent low compression. Changing winds and currents can sometimes produce a condition that seems, at first, power related.

I'll use the rest of the morning to fish and troll around in near-perfect sea conditions. My rationalization: trolling will put an engine through its paces at low power, not unlike extended cruising. Serendipitously, the salmon catch in the region has been unexpectedly good this year, and one of the best spots is right out Powell River's front door. Which is where I am, right now!

While killing time near Willingdon Beach, I cross behind the Texada Island ferry, the early-morning sun making beautiful contrasts on the water. The *Island Princess* can't enter the dock until the *Queen of Burnaby* exits for her run to Comox. Both ferries look stark 3-D in the low sun angle, but neither of them is bright white. Instead, large patches of rusty orange-brown cover extensive areas on the sides of both vessels. Supposedly, both ferries are soon to be retrofitted, so why paint them now? They're classic vessels that deserve a better appearance on their coastal runs.

Approaching the Hulks at the Mill Pond, I shift into idle-neutral, check the risers again, and rig up my fishing pole. I use a non-downrigger trolling setup, consisting of a big sinker, followed by a flasher, and finally a Coyote Wonderbread lure. The flasher I select has multicoloured spots, a nice match for the lure. It's Wonderbread all around.

Since it's unlikely I'll keep a salmon, even if I catch one, I pinch off the barb of the new lure. Because I'm a pure amateur at this sport, I don't usually troll expecting results. My only salmon in ten years on the coast was from *Mr. Bathtub* in shallow water at Bute Inlet. But today I have a good feeling. If nothing else, it'll be another enjoyable lollygag in the sun, so how can I go wrong?

I fish from the command bridge, so I can steer properly. Using the depth sounder, I try to keep in 150 to 180 feet of water, which is where recent salmon catches have been reported. The Mill is one of the hottest locations lately, so I aim at the tall non-functioning smokestack on shore, while lots of morning steam rises from the electrical powerplant farther inland.

Here comes the morning Pacific Coastal flight from Vancouver to Powell River, right on time. The Beechcraft 1900C turns final approach for Runway 09, passing directly behind me in its descent. It's nice to be so familiar with a community that you recognize when airline flights are on schedule. This same airplane will depart for Vancouver in another half-hour.

Approaching the Powell River paper mill

Several small boats troll near the mill, one coming towards me, closer to shore (in less than 150 feet depth), and I can see another bigger boat farther ahead. When I get closer to this larger vessel, I notice it's a commercial fishing boat, a good sign.

Commercial Ṭshing boat near the mill

My fishfinder is extremely active, nice big red fish icons at nearly all depths. They pop into view on the right side of the depth profile and frolic off the screen on the left. If these were real fish, they'd be jumping into my boat. Of course, I don't experience a single strike. But it's an entirely enjoyable experience, and today's expectation of maybe catching a salmon is worth the effort.

By the time I reach the river that feeds the powerplant (and sucks the water out of Powell Lake), it's time for the airline departure. The throaty turboprop should be impossible to miss, even though it will climb out behind me. But 9:10 comes and goes, and there's no departure. Oh, the wind is light from the east this morning, so the twin-Beechcraft has probably decided to save a few minutes on the flight to Vancouver by taking off to the east. More typically it's one way in (to the east) and the other way out (to the west), passing over the shoreline in both directions. The slightly uphill nature of Runway 09 and the more favourable terrain dropoff to the west usually determine the runway in use. But apparently not today.

At the river outlet, a red tin boat is trolling in a circular pattern, the lone occupant at the stern causing the boat to be highly angled upward at the bow. I expect he knows where to find fish. On the GPS, I notice a steep shelf dropping off here, which implies good fishing. So I ease my way towards the tin boat, keeping an appropriate distance away but seeking the same territory he's claimed.

As I approach the shallower area, the fisherman in the tin boat promptly retrieves his line and speeds away along the north shoreline, as if to say: "There's no fish here today."

In a few minutes, I decide he's right. I retrieve my line, and prepare to go.

One more test I want to conduct today involves fuel consumption. Before the recent valve replacements, consumption seemed extraordinarily high, and conditions are perfect today for an accurate test. My next stop will be Lund, where I'll refuel, so now I switch to the Bayliner's full auxiliary tank, and note the time. I'll promptly get up onto plane, and stay there at cruise for exactly 40 minutes, since I know the capacity of the aux tank will allow it. Then I'll switch back to the main tank for docking at Lund, and check the exact amount of fuel pumped into the auxiliary tank to refill it. The accuracy of such a test seems beyond dispute. If nothing else, it'll be nice to find a slight decrease in fuel consumption after the expensive repairs. And that's to be expected, considering the inefficiency of bad valves and low compression.

The trip to Lund will take less than 40 minutes, so I'll have an excuse to cruise past my destination and do a few wide circles near the Copeland Islands. On a perfect summer day like today, I'll use any opportunity for just bombing around in a boat of any size.

Sure enough, I come abeam Lund after only 32 minutes, make a few touring arcs, and wait for my watch to show 40 minutes. I come to a stop, switch tanks, and head towards the fuel dock.

My arrival at Lund doesn't mark the height of my boating skills. Turning around to position myself so my fuel tank fill inlets are closest to the dock, I shift in and out of both forward and reverse to make a smooth course reversal. All goes well until it's time for my final shift into forward. I misjudge my distance from the dock, and the boat's swim grid whacks against the railing. *Thunk!* No damage is done to either boat or the dock, but it identifies an imperfect arrival. Meanwhile, the fuel attendant is watching my every move, standing ready to help me with my lines. I look down at him from the command bridge as the Bayliner finally slides smoothly into place after the bounce off the swim grid.

"I'm here! Guess I didn't break anything."

He laughs, but I'm still embarrassed.

The fuel utilization test is a disappointment, indicating a higher rate of consumption than before the engine repairs. What I originally considered a well-controlled test, I now consider flawed, although I'm not sure what went wrong. I'll try another consumption test, and hope for better results.

When I go into the fuel office to pay my bill, I pass a new sign – at least it wasn't here when I visited a month ago: *Water – $10*. I consider asking the dock attendant if it's some kind of joke, but I know it isn't. So I let it go. Times are tough – water isn't free anymore, even in Canada.

After refueling, I move *Halcyon Days* over to the hotel dock, so I can go to shore for a late breakfast. I park near *Lazee Gal*, a vintage mahogany-and-white cruiser with Vancouver markings. This exquisite vessel could easily have been a major company yacht over fifty years ago. It doesn't take a lot of creativity to envision it traveling the Great Lakes as a presidential yacht. I have a very active imagination.

A woman is seated on the yacht's top deck, reading a book. I consider approaching her to ask about the history of the vessel. Then I remember how my privacy feels invaded when a lookie-loo cruises into Hole in the Wall. So I leave her alone, and snap a clandestine photo.

Old yacht at Lund

When I stop to visit Debra at her art shop, I find her at the front counter, with a customer in attendance at the other end of the store.

"Hi, Debra! I see our presidential yacht has arrived."

"What yacht?" she asks.

"The one at the hotel dock. What a beauty. We could have fun with that boat."

Debra walks out her front door, and looks down at the yacht. When she comes back inside, she asks the woman at the other end of the store: "Is that your boat?"

The woman says: "Yes," which opens my opportunity to ask my questions.

"I'm going to guess 1947," I say.

"Close. 1953," she replies

"Do you know it's previous history?"

"It's been in the family since it was built. So we inherited it."

"What a beauty."

But I'll still take *Halcyon Days*. After all, she's the almost-perfect boat.

Chapter 5

Boat Shopping

Although I don't know it at the time, this will be *Halcyon Days'* last summer in Westview's North Harbour. After spending most of the summer waiting for engine repairs, September finally provides some last-minute local cruising on the chuck before the marina is closed for a complete renovation. Over the winter, the North Harbour's docks will be disassembled, while new ones arrive on a huge barge.

The work goes to the lowest bidder in the States, and that doesn't please many of the local residents who want their marina constructed by Canadians. As I watch from my condo overlooking the harbour, the process proceeds ever so slowly, while I ponder whether the new marina will be open before next summer's recreational boating season.

Boats removed from the harbour are strewn throughout coastal British Columbia, many of them placed on blocks in driveways beside homes in Powell River. *Halcyon Days* is content to return to Powell

North Harbour construction

Lake to weather the winter in fresh water, docked at my cabin and operated occasionally for runs to town during weather that would otherwise challenge the Campion bowrider.

While the Bayliner spends this seasonal respite at the cabin, I look forward to many more years with this boat on the chuck, once the renovated harbour is complete. After all, *Halcyon Days* has a relatively new engine and a fresh new set of valves. All should settle down now with my "perfect boat."

Meanwhile, I'm spending more time in the States, since Margy's aging mother requires increased attention. Margy and I become hostage to Bellingham. It's a fine city, but it isn't Powell River. I'm determined to make the best of the situation, since the region is noted for it's outdoor recreational opportunities.

We transfer *Mr. Kayak*, our big yellow banana, to Bellingham, where we do several lengthy river trips, and I even begin writing a book on the subject (*Paddling the Pacific Northwest*). Margy and I begin to think about a purchasing a boat for Bellingham's harbour, to allow us to journey out onto the American chuck. With the San Juan Islands right in Bellingham's back yard, it seems a logical investment.

We refer to the prospective purchase of a U.S. boat as a "kick-around boat." It will be big enough to provide stability in good-weather cruises to the nearby islands, but purchased with a budget in mind. After all, the "perfect boat" remains in Powell River. This new craft will be used for exploring locally during visits to the States.

While I'm in Powell River, Margy finds a boat whose design appeals to her at a Bellingham boat dealer, but the salesman is hesitant to let her aboard. No, it isn't because she's a woman (not unheard of in boating communities, associating women aboard boats as bad luck), but because it has just arrived on the sales lot and needs cosmetic detailing. When I hear about the boat, I realize it's probably not the vessel for us, since it sounds in bad disrepair.

But a little elbow grease can turn a dirty boat into a buyer's dream. And that is what this 24-foot Bayliner becomes during our first visit together to the same boat a few weeks later. Margy is reluctant to even view the boat a second time, and I'm satisfied with looking at other boats instead. When it comes to vessels on the land, sea, or in the air, we're a couple who can rely on each other for nearly coinciding opinions regarding both design and function.

We go aboard the boat anyway, and immediately fall in love. Within another half hour, we're conferring with each other in the sales office.

"I suppose it's pretty stupid to make an offer on the first boat we lay eyes on," I say to Margy, while Geoff, the salesman, laughs at my attitude from behind his desk.

"Probably," replies Margy. "But it sure looks good now that it's cleaned up."

"Okay, I'm sold," I say. "Let's step outside together for a few minutes. Geoff, we'll be right back."

"Sure," says Geoff, in his easy-going manner.

Margy and I quickly learn that Geoff is always willing to accommodate our changes in direction when we get cranked up regarding boats. Over the next few months, we'll work closely with Geoff on two major boat purchases. This is the first.

Within a few minutes, we're back in his office. We make an offer, which is immediately accepted, and we're the proud owners of a 1995 Bayliner 2452, a sporty and fun-to-drive model I call a hardtop.

Bellingham Bayliner 2452

* * * * *

After a short test drive with Geoff, we sign the final paperwork, and we're off and running to explore the region by boat. Since this is still the winter-to-spring transition, we spend our first night in the V-berth tied up to the dock in Bellingham, where we use an electric heater to keep us warm.

We venture a few miles down the coast to Chuckanut Bay, anchoring alongside the train trestle, and then into Rosario Strait and out to the San Juan Islands. We dock at Friday Harbor, where the female fuel attendant seems to misunderstand my sense of humour when I kid Margy about how quiet this marina is.

"Probably just like this during the summer," I say, making sure the attendant overhears me as I pump the gas.

"Not quite," she interjects.

I give her my surprised look. Friday Harbor is, of course, well-known as one of the biggest summertime boating zoos of the entire region.

* * * * *

A few days after our visit to Friday Harbor, I take my friend Jeanne on her first ride in the new (to me) boat. Jeanne is an acknowledged white-knuckle passenger in anything on wheels or wings. But she's perfectly comfortable whipping through big waves in a little boat, even with a novice like me at he helm. I give her a chance to drive the boat at slow speeds, although I'm hesitant. During her first chance at the wheel, she looks serious and determined, slow and careful about every move. This is a good start.

I want her introduction to this boat to be memorable (in a good sort of way), so we retrace the path I've recently traveled to Friday Harbor, a route that feels comfortable. We stop along the way at Spencer Spit, where I demonstrate how enjoyable a tranquil bay can be, tied up to a mooring buoy and basking in the spring sun.

All goes well, until I give her the chance to drive the boat at higher speeds. She controls the boat nicely during cruise, and responds well to my instructions regarding adjustments to the trim tabs and heading to keep us away from the rocks and shallow water that's clearly labeled on the GPS.

Although there are few boats out today, we encounter two headed towards us as we approach a fairly narrow passage between two islands.

Jeanne driving the Bayliner 2452

The first is small runabout, speeding along at a fair clip, followed by a bigger (and slower) recreational trawler, maybe a Nordic Tug. Both have deviated to the north side of the passage, and I instruct Jeanne to take a heading that will allow us to pass well to their south, but not so close to shore that it will cause problems. The island on our side looks clear of rocks, and the water is deep, so this should work out well. Still, I tell her to keep her hand on the throttle, and be ready to slow down and deviate closer to the island as the boats get nearer.

We meet the first boat just before we enter the passage, and its wake is inconsequential. But the second vessel is going to be a challenge, since we'll meet it directly between the islands, with little maneuvering space to stay comfortably away from shore.

Jeanne's hand is on the throttle, and she's reacting well to each minor change in heading I recommend. But I'm getting nervous about our closeness to shore.

"As soon as we pass behind this boat, turn slightly away from shore, to give us plenty of clearance from the island."

"Okay," she replies.

And she does just as I instruct, turning to starboard as we pass the trawler. I see the wake approaching us, but it doesn't look very substantial. But I'm also not familiar with how much rough water our new Bayliner can take at this speed. I misjudge, and we pay the consequences.

The wake is a sudden jolt that sends us airborne. I'm standing beside Jeanne when she goes flying up from her meagerly supported captain's chair, a lightly braced structure that's suffered nearly two decades of all-weather exposure to the elements. The open-air design behind the boat's helm provides plenty of fresh air, but it has led to years of dry rot in the base of the chair. When Jeanne comes back down, the seat collapses.

"Whack!" goes the chair as it comes apart at its base, sending shards of dark, damp wood all over the back deck. Jeanne, now leaning forward against the wheel, immediately reduces the throttle to idle, and we bob in the passing wake of the trawler.

One of the two metal mounts connecting the chair to the gunnel is twisted severely, so the remains of the chair lie precariously tilted and totally unusable. Fortunately, neither of us is injured, and the boat can easily be driven from a standing position for the rest of the day. But the destroyed seat not a pretty sight. We're both laughing, which is a good thing.

"When we get to Friday Harbor, I'll find a wrench and pull the chair completely off the wall," I say. "For now, just ignore it."

"I told you not to trust me with machinery," Jeanne laughingly replies.

"Why don't you let me drive for now," I add.

"Sounds appropriate to me."

The perfect introductory cruise has suddenly taken a turn for the worse, but we're two people who can find joy in a botched adventure. There's no reason to turn around and head home just because of a broken chair.

When I dock at Friday Harbor, the same female fuel attendant meets our boat. I can't help but kid around with her while I pump the gas.

"We're what's known as amateur boaters," I say, as I notice her glancing inside at the aft deck and the splinters of damp wood, with the twisted captain's chair drooping dramatically from its single sidewall attachment fitting.

She says nothing, and I don't explain.

A few minutes later, we're motoring to the adjacent transient parking finger, where Margy and I docked only a few days before. It was narrow between the dock and shore then, and now it's even tighter. For one thing, the row of boats is longer, and I'll need to parallel park between two of them. And the tide is a lot lower. In fact, this is a negative tide, and the transient dock is in a challenging position, close to the shore.

I notice the water appears a lot muddier than on my previous visit, and I can see bottom. But I want to swing fairly close to shore to give myself room to turn around and parallel park. Before I notice just how shallow it is, I feel a thump, as the skeg of the stern-drive (and maybe the prop) hits bottom.

Luckily, I'm in idle when this occurs, and I immediately shift into neutral. I'm reasonably certain there's been no damage, but the skeg of the leg has firmly implanted itself in the mucky bottom.

I turn off the engine, and try to push away from shore with a pike pole, but the bottom is so soft the pole simply pushes into the muck without any effect. We are firmly stuck. And from what I remember of the tide tables, the water is still on its way down.

I look around. Jeanne is giggling, which is a lot better than being upset. I'm not giggling at all, but I'm surprised to see no one shouting suggestions from shore or intervening, as I would normally expect in a major marina like this. I look up at the small shack where the fuel attendant waits for arriving boats. She isn't visible, but I visualize her looking out at us and laughing from behind her closed door.

"I'm going out onto the swim grid to use the kicker," I explain to Jeanne.

"Okay," she says, without further comment. I'm not sure she even knows what a kicker is, but I take no time to explain.

I quickly connect the cruise-a-day to the Honda outboard, and the small motor fires up almost immediately. Thank goodness for electric starters on outboards.

Shifting into gear, alternately forward and then reverse, does nothing. I gun the kicker, but we don't move. Then I hear a calm but knowledgeable voice yelling over to me from the dock.

"Can I give you a hand?" says a thin, bearded fellow who looks like he knows boats. "If you can toss me a heaving line, I'll pull you out of there." Then he adds: "Lots of folks get stuck here. It's a low-low tide, and a bad spot that should be marked better."

His last sentence is the most important one, for it reassures me I might not be ridiculed for my stupid mistake of going aground in an established marina. It should be a small part of what's happening, but it makes me feel a lot better immediately.

When I step into the cabin to look for a heaving line, I realize I don't' have one. In fact, I have no long ropes on board, which is an obvious omission for a safe and knowledgeable boater. When I step back onto the aft deck, I have no excuses.

"Sorry," I yell to the man. "I don't have a long rope at all."

"No problem," he replies. "They'll have one on the sheriff's boat."

He steps onto the aft deck of the nearby sheriff's skookum metal boat, and almost immediately produces a coiled rope that he tosses to me. On the first throw, I fail to catch the rope, and it falls into the water next to us. The bearded man retrieves the rope quickly, and tosses it again. I catch it easily this time, and start to wrap it around the cleat on the starboard side of the stern.

"Take it around to the bow, if you can," he says.

I quickly navigate the narrow catwalk to the bow, and attach the rope to a cleat. The man begins to pull, and the bow swings smartly towards him, and then continues to move slowly but surely towards the dock. The stern-drive's skeg pull off the bottom, and we swing smoothly into deeper water, out of harm's way.

"I can start the engine now," I say. "It's deep enough here. Do you think it's okay to park on the other side of the dock?"

"Sure," the man replies. "They should have told you to park there in the first place. It's too shallow on this side."

Once again, he's reassured me that it's not all my fault. Of course, I know it is.

The engine starts nicely, so I disconnect the heaving line and slowly motor around to the other side of the dock, where a wide-open spot awaits me. When I come up against the dock, the man takes the line I offer to him and ties me up to the railing.

"Anything else I can do?" he asks.

Now I realize he's looking straight in at me and Jeanne, where we stand near a pile of wooden shards and a seat twisted like its been in a train wreck.

"No. We're okay now, thanks to you."

As the man walks away, he says nothing about the smashed seat, but he adds: "No big deal. We've all been there at one time or the other. Now have yourselves a nice day."

* * * * *

THE NEW BAYLINER 2452 is such a fun boat in the waters around Bellingham that we briefly (but not seriously) discuss swapping it with the Bayliner in Powell River. Both are 24 feet in length, resulting in moderate stability in rough water, and both have a similar engine, but the 2452 gets up onto plane quicker and cruises a few knots faster. We're amazed that the view from the slightly raised helm is so good, nearly as encompassing as the view from a command bridge. Although we're not serious about the swap (especially considering border crossing and re-registration), it does give us cause to think about our "perfect boat" back in Powell River. Maybe it's not so perfect, after all.

Imagine, instead, a bigger version of *Halcyon Days*, maybe with a length of 28 or 30 feet. And the time for buying a boat is favorable – boats have come down a lot in price in recent years. To call it a buyer's market is to say the very least.

We thus begin to search for a replacement for *Halcyon Days*, and we turn to Geoff for assistance. We start with a list of mandatory items, and add a lengthy list of desired equipment. We set a budgetary target, and begin focusing on the exact makes and models we want to investigate. Three top models head the list. All are Bayliners, admittedly not because they're the best boat on the water, but because you get a lot of boat for your money. The three prime candidates are the Bayliner 3058 (30-footer, command bridge, twin engines), the 2858 (28-footer of similar design but typically equipped with a single engine), and the unusual 2859 (the 28-foot big daddy version of our new Bellingham boat, also equipped with a single engine). The possibility of twin engines, while remaining within our budgetary constraints, becomes an overwhelming passion for me. We narrow our search to the Bayliner 3058.

This model was constructed for only three years, 1991 – 93, and one of the first boats we're attracted to is a 1993 model, which many consider ugly by comparison to its 1991 – 92 brethren. However, we like the lines of the boat, and it's a full foot wider than the earlier years, which is a definite plus. We meet Dick in LaConner, just south of Bellingham, and we're overwhelmed with the wider 3058 he uses as an office when he's in town, venturing out for occasional leisurely cruises.

Dick builds boats for a living – skookum welded aluminum crew boats that can be converted to recreational cruisers. His fellow workers kid him about owning a Bayliner, a product many look down on as the "cheap" boat on the block.

"I couldn't afford one of the boats I build," he explains. "So I bought this one instead. Lots of people call Bayliners crappy boats, but you sure get a lot of crap for your money."

It's true – this model Bayliner comes equipped with features I could never afford from another builder. I'll take a lot of nice crap every time.

One of the few drawbacks is Dick's engine package, which deviates from the typical twin 5.0-litre Mercruisers. His boat has twin 4.3-litre engines, and that provides both pluses and minuses. The biggest drawback is the difficulty in getting up on plane, which means little to Dick, since he uses his boat for slow-speed gunkholing.

"It'll get up onto plane, but not when the hull and legs are covered with heavy marine growth," says Dick, which is the normal state of affairs in the waters of the narrow channel flowing through LaConner.

In fact, the boat is about to be hauled out for its annual hull and leg cleaning. So Dick, in his normal truthfulness (which doesn't include any glitzy boat salesmanship), suggests we wait for a sea demonstration until the cleaning is complete. He's insistent that a clean hull will allow this boat to plane. Since a planing hull is on the mandatory page of our list of features, maybe this isn't the engine configuration for us.

But along with the borderline planing issue is the fuel efficiency side of the coin. This boat should be particularly economical, if it can get onto the step without demanding full power from the 4.3-litre

Mercs. And when you pop open the engine compartment, there's space to spare on all sides. Compared to twin 5.0-litre engines, this boat should be a mechanic's joy (which can lead to an owner's joy).

We're serious enough about this boat that we visit LaConner the next week to see the Bayliner again when it's on blocks at the local shipyard, getting its hull and legs pressure washed. We're even more impressed the second time around, although we haven't yet left the dock.

Dick's 1993 Bayliner 3058 at LaConner, Washington

But Geoff has found another 3058 in Richmond, BC, a 1992 model. The location is particularly attractive, since we would be buying a Canadian boat that wouldn't need to be imported. Richmond is within close reach of Bellingham (by car) and Powell River (by Pacific Coastal to Vancouver's South Terminal), so I visit the boat one day when I'm driving to Bellingham after my airline arrival from Powell River. On my regular drive south, I pass over the middle arm of the Fraser River, within sight of Skyline Marina, so it's an easy place to stop. It doesn't take long to fall in love with this 3058. What seals the deal is the remote-controlled windlass, along with the digital fuel flow meters at both the upper and lower helms.

"Does the remote control for the anchor operate?" I ask Philip, the boat salesman who sits next to me on the command bridge.

"Let's give it a try," he says, pushing the "down" button.

I watch the anchor ride immediately down a few feet, easily visible from up here. Then he releases the switch, hits the "up" button, and the anchor retracts back into its original position. I imagine myself pulling into a bay in a distant inlet during one of my beloved solo voyages. What a way to anchor!

I report my fascination with this boat to Margy, who agrees to purchase it sight-unseen, based on my perceptions and a few photos. She understands my enthrallment with the remote windlass, having been through many frustrating anchoring experiences with me.

We begin the purchase paperwork, even before Margy pays a visit to the boat the following week following a Powell River trip. Not unexpectedly, her impressions of the boat are the same as mine – this is our new "perfect boat."

1992 Bayliner 3058 at Richmond, British Columbia

* * * * *

THINGS PROCEED RAPIDLY. We meet Geoff in Richmond, along with a hired marine surveyor and a mechanic who will help us make the final purchase decision. The surveyor and mechanic crawl all over the boat, working together to check out the engines, hull, and accessories. Then we all go out for a sea trial, with Geoff at the command bridge helm.

Geoff at helm of Bayliner 3058 in Richmond

I watch closely as Geoff maneuvers out of the tight confines of Skyline Marina. He keeps the wheel centered, while working the two shift levers and throttles with his hands flying from one lever to another. It's a left-right-swing-reverse ballet, and I'm impressed with the maneuverability of a twin-screw boat. I also ponder whether I'll be able to quickly adjust to the new concepts involving two-engine docking. There may be a significant learning curve, and the close confines of this tightly spaced urban marina makes me nervous.

Once out on the middle arm of the Fraser, we motor slowly north under the twin bridges, and then left at the bigger bridge that marks the outlet to the north arm. Although Geoff has never boated in this area, he quickly adjusts.

"How soon can I open 'er up?" he asks the mechanic.

"Once you're abeam that barge terminal on your right, you can give it a go," replies the mechanic.

During the no-wake dance on the way out of the confines of the marina and bridges, we bob side-to-side at the upper helm. I don't even notice it until Margy mentions the motion.

"Kinda tipsy up here," she says.

"A little," I reply. "But there's five of us today, so that gives us a pretty high center of gravity."

Geoff nods in agreement, and no one says anything else about it, until we start up onto plane.

"Here we go," announces Geoff, as he pours the coals to the 3058.

Full throttle seems to come awfully quickly, but I'm sure he's pushing the engines a bit hard on purpose. If something bad is going to show up, a sea trial is the place you should find it.

It isn't the noise of the full-throttle twin engines that impresses me the most. It isn't even the obviously powerful forward momentum. Instead, it's the deck angle, which jumps upward steeply. And it's the side-to-side sway at this high angle that scares me the most.

"Damn it!" yells Geoff, working the wheel and the trim tabs, trying to stop the pendulous sway, but not coming back even a bit on the throttles. "Come on baby!"

Geoff is determined to get us up onto plane, come hell or high water. I'm worried about the high water.

My first thought is we're going swimming, unless Geoff comes back on the power soon. The lateral movement is impossible to catch with the trim tabs. Just as Geoff attempts to adjust the tabs, we start swinging the other way, making matters worse.

My second thought is I'm not wearing a life jacket. Sure, the water isn't outrageously cold in May, and the bank of the river is only about 50 metres away, but I'm not used to being in a boat without wearing a preserver. Of course, none of us are wearing a life preserver, and I don't recall even seeing any on board during our earlier survey of the boat.

"You'd better come back on the power," the mechanic says calmly.

"You're right, I'll have to," replies Geoff, as he finally reduces the throttles.

The boat immediately returns to thankful stability.

"Maybe a few of us ought to go below," says the marine surveyor, heading for the stairs.

In fact, we all go below now, and Geoff uses the lower helm to bring the previous bronco of a boat smoothly up on plane, with hardly any need for the trim tabs. We slow to a stop near a line of luxury houses on the north shore of the river, and then turn around and power-up again as we cruise back to Skyline at 25 knots. The boat handles fine now that our crew's weight is in the lower cabin. I take the helm for a short time, amazed at the power of the twin engines. But there's a major lesson here that should be no surprise – a thousand pounds of people on the top deck is obviously beyond the throttle-up capabilities of this boat.

As we approach Skyline Marina from the north side, Geoff aims at the haul-out dock, where the Bayliner will go into a sling for a ride upward and out of the water for a pressure wash and a close look at the hull and legs. These inspections, along with the previous checks by the mechanic and marine surveyor, pronounce the boat as ready to

In the sling for inspection

purchase. We'll need to await the results of the engine oil samples, but there's really no doubt.

After an exciting hour in the sling, the boat is back in the water. We say our goodbyes to the mechanic and marine surveyor, and Geoff drives the 3058 back to our slip, where I ask Geoff to back the boat into position.

"You want to see how easy it is to back up with twin engines?" he asks.

"Not really," I reply. "This place scares me. When I'm ready to leave this dock without you, I want a straight-forward shot out to the river. I plan on one left turn out of this slip, then a right turn to go under the bridge. Then I'll be headed for Powell River, and I ain't comin' back."

Chapter 6

Anchor Freefall

While construction continues in Powell River's North Harbour, Margy and I spend Victoria Day weekend in Richmond, working on cleanup projects in our new boat, and venturing out twice to test systems. For both excursions, we closely watch the tides. Even though we travel only near slack water, the current in the river never seems to slow down, contorting through the docks every which way.

Our first trip is in the early evening, coinciding with a high tide. Besides serving as an attempt to learn how to maneuver the boat, we have another goal. As densely populated as the marina slips in Vancouver may be, there are few pump-out stations. But at the outlet to the north arm of the Fraser, we can proceed three miles offshore to the legal sewage discharge limit, and use our macerator to dump our holding tank, which seems full. (Later we realize the transparent tank that appears full is really the drinking water tank, but this trip seems necessary at the time.)

Thanks to Geoff, we're pointed bow-out. So it will be merely a left turn and straight into the river, which looks easy. Of course, I'm already violating my resolve to make only one straight-out departure from this dock (to travel to Powell River), and I'm obviously not experienced enough to attempt backing this boat into its slip upon our return. And I quickly find that even this straight-forward departure holds its challenges. The ever-changing Fraser, even near slack tide, simply refuses to cooperate.

With my limited twin-engine experience (except in airplanes, which incorporate brakes for control when taxiing), Margy and I decide it will be wise to position her on the bow, pike pole at the ready to push off any boats that we approach too close. Up on the command bridge, when the engines are warm, I shift into forward on the right engine, leaving the left in neutral. The boat reacts as expected, easing to the left just as planned. But as soon as the bow enters the waterway between the fingers, the river's current (compounded by the incoming tide) catches us, and pushes the bow back to the right. I add a touch of reverse on the left engine, which also produces the reaction I expect. But the overall current is still pushing us towards the boat directly across the waterway. Aboard this neighboring boat, I notice a figure in the cabin who seems to be preparing his dinner on the stove, with his back turned to our approaching Bayliner and its protruding anchor platform.

Margy waves her left arm outward, indicating I should be turning in that direction. I'm trying, and even have the controls in the correct position (right shift lever forward, left in reverse). But still we drift towards the unsuspecting dinner-preparing boater. What's needed is a touch of throttle on both engines. But with Margy standing on the bow, I'm afraid to power up too fast.

Margy waves her left arm frantically now, so I add some power on both engines (starboard, more forward thrust; port, more reverse). The boat reacts, and so does Margy. She stumbles, but quickly regains her footing. Whew! – we swing past the nearby boat's stern, clearing it by less than a metre, and Margy is still on her feet. Then we're suddenly free of obstacles, and on our way.

"We must have given that guy quite a scare," Margy says, when she joins me on the command bridge.

"I saw him in the cabin, but then I lost track of him. Things were happening awfully fast."

"The last I saw of that guy, he was staring back at us, probably waiting for the collision."

We're out in the river now, where there's lots of room to maneuver. We pass under the twin bridges, still only slightly above idle. The boat handles well with both engines in forward and low power. At the big bridge, we turn left and down the north arm of the Fraser. Passing the barge terminal, I keep the engines at low power, enjoying the scenery and the feel of the boat. A few minutes later, I hand over the helm to

Margy, and she continues slowly down the river, looking comfortable at the controls.

Besides our plan to use the macerator pump once we're sufficiently offshore, it's early enough in the day to either come back up the river to Skyline Marina for the night or continue to English Bay for an overnight stay. Better yet, because of the reported poor anchor holding conditions in English Bay, we'll evaluate the situation once we're clear of the Fraser, and maybe continue into False Creek. We have lots of options and lots of time to try our first on-plane operation, so there's no need to hurry down the river. It's that kind of a late May day, approaching sunset– hazy sun and lazy boaters ambling slowly down the river, with lots of evening twilight to spare.

About 45 minutes after leaving the dock, with Margy still driving, we're approaching the jetty that marks the mouth of the north arm, still traveling slowly. Vancouver Airport is now behind us on our left, and the open water beyond looks tranquil. It's only then that we recognize we may be in trouble.

"Take a look at that," says Margy, pointing to the fuel flow indicator.

The indicator is a multi-meter digital display that shows the combined flow of both engines at the top of the gauge. I've been watching this display for the past half hour as Margy drives, and it shows a fluctuating number that seems to average 11 gallons per hour. This makes sense to me – inefficiently plowing water at a slow speed with the combined power of both engines well below their normal cruise setting. There are other digits at the bottom of the gauge that I haven't paid any attention to, and on the right side of the display is a vertical bar, mostly white with a small black strip at the bottom. Below the bar are the words "Total Fuel."

"Does that mean we're almost out of gas?" asks Margy in a tone of concern.

"No, we've got plenty of gas," I reply. "The analog gauge at the lower helm shows half full."

"Well, which is right?" she asks.

Good point. I was surprised the former owner of this boat would leave us with a half full tank of fuel. At today's soaring fuel price, that equates to about $300 worth of gas, a nice gift, if it's accurate.

"The gauge downstairs is the best indicator," I say. "This one has to be properly set to have any meaning."

I'm being truthful with her, as far as I know, but my doubts have suddenly been raised. Until now, I saw only the traditional analog (needle) gauge downstairs, and it clearly indicated a half tank of fuel. From my flying background in our Piper Arrow, I'm familiar with fuel flow gauges (although not digital ones). In the Arrow, the gauge doesn't even feed off actual fuel flow. Instead, it taps fuel pressure, and then converts it to fuel flow for the cockpit display. Probably this boat merely computes fuel remaining by clocking the fuel flow and displaying it as total quantity in the tank. Most likely (I hope), you need to reset the fuel flow gauge each time you refuel to make the now-mostly-white bar anywhere near accurate. But right in front of me is an indication we may be almost out of gas.

At the bottom of the indicator is another digital window. This one is labeled "Fuel Remaining," and it reads "8.15 gallons." Eight gallons on twin engine 5.0-litre engines is as close to "none" as I ever want to get in this boat.

"I'll check downstairs again," I say, leaving Margy at the upstairs helm.

When I arrive at the lower helm, the duplicate fuel-flow gauge (same as the upper helm) indicates the same out-of-gas condition. But the old-fashioned needle gauge is fluctuating back and forth near the half-tank line. It's a good sign. The needle is moving rather than completely stationary, which might otherwise mean totally inoperative. But which indicator do I believe? The digital readout on the command bridge says nearly "zero," and it's the higher-tech gauge of the two. Yet this older analog indicator is a usually-reliable, stupid-simple float system. Of course, things can go dramatically wrong with these old gauges now and then. I hope it isn't now.

I climb back up to join Margy, and tell her what I found below.

"It's a half-tank, I'm sure."

I explain my theory about the digital fuel flow gauge not being reset at the last refuel. She follows my argument, but she's no more certain of the real amount of gas than I am. One thing almost for sure – we either have a half tank or almost none.

"Let's turn around, and start back up the river, just in case," I say.

In reality, it's more than an instance of just-in-case. There's no fuel anywhere near our current location, so the only logical and safe solution is to return to our dock. By now it's after 6 o'clock, so there's no answer when I phone the fuel dock near Skyline Marina. The voicemail, however, has a "Push 5" selection for those in need of emergency assistance. I make note of the 5-selection, and tuck my cell phone into my pocket, where it will be ready to dial in case things get suddenly quiet. The river, ever roiling, is cooperating at the moment, except for its constant downstream flow. If we have to run out of gas, it's a nice evening to do it.

"What do you want me to do about the throttles?" asks Margy.

Once again, I revert back to my experience with airplanes.

"A low power setting is definitely better, although it'll take longer to get back to the dock. If this were an airplane, we'd reduce to best rate of climb speed."

"Well, that helps a lot," laughs Margy.

Even in a desperate situation, we keep a happy face, at least most of the time. To me, tonight, it seems more funny than serious. To Margy, it's a bit more dour. Still, she keeps up her spirit, which helps keep up mine, too.

We settle in at 1300 RPM on both engines, a number that keeps us moving upstream against the current, but not so slow that getting back to our dock seems to take forever. As I remind Margy, we also have a full cruise-a-day for the 5-horsepower outboard motor for our dinghy. Although there's no kicker bracket on the transom, we could launch the dinghy, attach the outboard, and get a few extra miles by using the dinghy to push ourselves back to Skyline Marina. Of course, we've never launched the dinghy, nor started the 5-horse outboard. But having an alternative perks us up. So we try to laugh our way back up the river.

About 30 minutes later, we can see the big bridge, and the vertical bar on the fuel flow gauge is almost entirely white, with just a touch of black at the bottom. The "Fuel Remaining" window slips below "4.00 gallons." My gut feeling is we're probably going to make it.

With a mere 1.73 gallons remaining (or else nearly a half tank), we pull into our slip, with a surprisingly smooth approach and arrival. It's true that our protruding inflatable dinghy (mounted on the swim grid) fends off the neighbouring boat with a slight bounce, but I consider it an overall successful docking. And we didn't run out of fuel! Of course, we didn't get to use our macerator pump either.

* * * * *

THE NEXT DAY, after spending the night in the V-berth, we're ready to go again. I've now read the brochure that discusses the fuel flow gauge. Sure enough, the gauge must be reset after each refuel in order to provide an accurate fuel quantity reading. Our plan is to go to the nearby fuel dock for gas, and then out to the confluence of the middle and north arms to practice docking at the River Rock Marina, and then test the electric windlass for the first time. Though I don't want to drop the anchor all the way to the bottom of this river (way too much discarded junk, including old cars, as I visualize it). But we can at least carefully test the remote operation of the windlass. The plan is to lower the anchor only a few metres, and then retrieve it.

This time, we'll be backing out into the narrow waterway as we depart. It doesn't go perfect, but it a big improvement over the previous day. I conclude that our parking spot is better suited to an easy exit using reverse throttle (on one side, of course) rather than trying to leave while parked facing straight out. This time, I back out into the combined current and wind, and the stern swings around efficiently until I'm nearly aligned with the waterway and properly poised for exit.

At the empty fuel dock, I make a fairly good arrival. We take on 71 gallons of gas to top off the 125 gallon tank, proof positive that the old analog fuel gauge in the lower helm is within its expected level of accuracy. I reset the digital fuel flow gauge, and get a full black vertical bar. Then we restart the engines and proceed north below the dual spans to the wide-open area where the arms of the river join.

To our right, the docks of River Rock Casino are a perfect spot to practice docking. The entire outside edge of the outermost finger is clear of boats. It makes the perfect place to learn to maneuver.

Headed out the north arm of the Fraser River

However, with the strong flow of the Fraser, I need repeated attempts to get properly positioned, and always end up a full boat width from the dock. At least I don't hit anything.

Satisfied that I've had some decent practice, we head back out into the wide-open area for some windlass practice.

"We won't drop the anchor all the way," I say to Margy. "And with this kind of current, we may have to drop it while holding a little power into the flow, rather than in idle. Do you feel comfortable doing that while I go up to the bow to make sure the chain is free and goes down clean?"

"Sure," she says, meaning she'd rather operate the engines and the windlass from the command bridge than climb out to the bow, which is not her favourite thing. We know our appropriate places, and when anchoring, with or without a windlass, this is the way we do it.

At the bow, I open the rode locker, where a huge pile of rope is stored. I still don't understand how the chain will transfer to the rope in the windlass, but it all certainly looks tidy. The rope winds out of the topside locker and into a cylindrical chamber, while the chain comes directly up from another locker below.

Meanwhile, Margy is fighting the current, but keeping the boat straight and relatively stationary with a little power on both engines. I motion to her, pointing down with my thumb, and she hits the remote switch. The anchor starts down slowly, and I watch the chain ride smoothly through the gears of the windlass.

"Stop!" I yell, while making a cut-off signal across my throat with my hand.

The anchor stops, now barely in the water. I notice it's being pushed back towards the bow by the strong flow of the river.

"A little less throttle!" I yell.

Margy correctly interprets my instructions, and the anchor and its chain now ride nearly vertical. I motion downward again with my thumb, and the windlass unwinds some more.

"Stop!" I yell again, not sure how far below the water the anchor now rides, but it can't be over 10 feet down. The windlass stops again, just as advertised.

"Down again!" I yell, while motioning with my thumb again.

Once again, the windlass begins its efficient anchor-down rotation. Then all hell breaks loose! Suddenly, and completely without warning, the windlass begins to spin at an increasing rate. I can hear the heavy chain flying through the sprocket, speeding up even more as the windlass spins. I step back from the bow, wondering if something is going to fly apart, throwing my arms up into the sky in defeat. Zing! – something fairly large flies off the spinning windlass on the starboard side, splashing far out in the water to our right.

The chain continues to unwind. I never would have guessed there was this much chain in the locker. It seems at least 100 feet have left the bow, and then I see the first part of the rope start to move. With a resounding crunching sound, the windlass freezes, with the rope jammed in the sprocket.

Now what? Pulling the heavy chain up may be impossible by hand. Certainly more chain has been deployed than necessary to reach the bottom of the river. If I can pull it up by hand, I'll reach the point where the anchor finally leaves the bottom of the river. I doubt I'll be able to handle it any farther, considering the weight of the anchor and the remaining chain. It looks like we'll need to get on the radio, and call for help. Then what? – Is there any alternative to cutting the rope and leaving the chain and anchor (expensive!) on the bottom of the river?

Meanwhile, Margy has been startled enough to loose some of her lateral control. We've wandered off to the left and are sitting cockeyed relative to the extended chain. Simultaneously, we're sliding backwards and away from the anchor.

"Come forward, slowly!" I yell back to her.

She quickly regains control of the boat. Taking her cues from my hand signals, she brings the boat back to the point where the chain hangs nearly vertical under the bow.

"I'm going to try to pull it up! Do your best to keep us over this spot!"

"Okay!" she yells back.

In just a few minutes, I'm exhausted, and I've retrieved only a few metres of chain, piling it on the bow near the rode locker.

"Try the drum winch!" yells Margy.

Why not? The foot switch is right there, and maybe the drum will accept chain as well as rope. Sure enough – it works! Slowly but surely I retrieve the chain, with the pile on the bow growing ever higher. And now the increased tension indicates the anchor itself is coming up.

I don't really understand what has happened. The foot switch for the rotating drum is working fine, and the chain rides upward on the drum with a little extra pull from me to prevent slippage. The seized windlass with its jammed rope shouldn't allow the drum to rotate, since they're on the same shaft. The windlass shaft has sheared, sending the anchor into freefall and launching the clutch nut off into the water. Yet the broken shaft is what allows the drum to rotate when I push the foot switch (good). Even though the windlass is jammed with the rope, This freak chain of events allows me to retrieve the chain and anchor. In other words, it's a mix of good and bad, but at least we're detached from the river bottom, and able to motor back to our dock unassisted.

So in three brief trips in this new (to us) boat, we almost flip over during the test ride, come close to bashing into a boat where the captain is cooking dinner, nearly run out of gas (or so we thought), fail to empty our holding tank (which we erroneously thought was full), destroy our windlass, and nearly lose our anchor and all of its chain. But we have learned a lot – the hard way.

Anchor chain on bow

Chapter 7

North to Powell River

A new boat is an exciting thing to behold. No matter how big or small, no matter how expensive, no matter what the weather, you remember your first real voyage in a new vessel. Going north and home to Powell River fit those parameters. The test runs on the Fraser River, although all too exciting, were not a cruise. The trip home, however, meets the criteria of a first voyage.

The plan is to bring the boat north as soon as the anchor windlass is repaired and the new marina opens at Westview Harbour. Considering the latest view from my condo in Powell River (overlooking the docks), that trip might not occur during June. While the boat repair shop in Richmond works on the windlass, progress on marina construction seems to be in slow motion. The new cement docks are mostly in place, but the details are proceeding at what seems a snail's pace. Boards are strewn on the docks, rafts are tied up here and there, and the pile-driving crane is still working on the bigger slips at the entrance end of the marina. Jim, the wharfinger, is his normal cheerful self, but I can see through his disguise. There's lots of pressure from local boaters about details beyond his control. He manages the marina, not the process of construction.

A letter arrives announcing the marina opening date – June 13th. That seems optimistic, but I enthusiastically mark it on my calendar, along with my newly assigned dock location. A week later, the bill for moorage arrives, noting that my payment date begins June 16th. I take that to mean the opening date may be slipping, and City Hall is trying to keep the hounds at bay. That's not easy to do in this town.

I come down the lake from my cabin on June 12th, a Sunday, one day before the originally announced opening date. From my condo balcony, things don't look promising. A large construction raft blocks the spot where I'm supposed to park, and a big crane is positioned at the harbour entrance. No boats will be coming in for a while. With the windlass repairs in Richmond now complete, I wait a few more days before phoning Jim.

"Hey, Wayne, I need to ask you to make it kinda quick," says Jim in what seems to be an artificially calm voice. "I've got an office full of people."

I can picture the scene – probably a room full of irate locals, each with their own private gripe, as if the wharfinger has control over the construction process. It's hard to get Jim riled, but I can see how this could do it to anyone.

I briefly explain: "I'm planning to go down to Richmond to prepare my new boat for the trip north, if you think I'll be able to get into the new harbour in a few days."

"Well, right now there's too much construction going on to open the harbour as we planned," says Jim. "But it looks promising for later in the week. I'd just hate to see you get all the way up here and not be able to get in."

"I promise to stay flexible. It'll take Margy and me a day to get to Richmond, and then we'll start north slowly, enjoying ourselves along the way. When you're open, we'll come in. Until then, we'll just cruise."

"Good. Gotta go now, Wayne. Things are hoppin' here this morning."

Hopping is one way to explain it. I bet it's more like controlled chaos.

* * * * *

IN RICHMOND, MARGY AND I SPEND TWO NIGHTS on the boat, awaiting better weather. The skies are clearing, but there's a strong northwest wind. The Fraser River flows every which way, and once we exit the north arm, the waves will be even worse than in this sheltered location. As has been proven to me many times before, there's a lot of good everywhere, and Margy and I thoroughly enjoy our unexpected extra days in Richmond. But it does pose a small problem regarding our plans for traveling north.

Margy needs to get back to Bellingham by Friday, so the delay at Richmond means we'll need to head to Powell River without a lot of stops along the way. In fact, it would be best if we did the trip as a one-day shot when the winds subside (which is the forecast for Thursday). It's 130 kilometres, not including course changes along the coast, but it can be done in a day. So much for a leisurely trip.

The new plan is to get up early on Thursday, departing when the Fraser River is at high tide. Currents will be minimum then, and the winds are forecast to be light. If the new harbour is still not able to accept incoming boats when we arrive, I can drop Margy at the Powell River fuel dock, so she can hop on the next day's Pacific Coastal flight to Vancouver, and then drive to Bellingham from there. Meanwhile, I'll cruise around, overnighting at some of the local anchorages until the harbour is open. After all, it's already past the original opening date, and even beyond the initial moorage billing date (which will have the locals in a tizzy). Jim's office is most likely a constant parade of whiners. So much so that I'm nervous even phoning him.

"Hey, Jim, I bet you're having fun today," I say when he answers the telephone.

"Oh, sure. A real bag full of fun."

"That's what I figured. Anyway, I wanted to see when you expect I'll be able to come into the harbour."

"We're open for harbour traffic now from 5 pm until 7 am, every day. Just don't come in before five or the crane will be blocking the entrance. They tend to get pretty upset when boats try to sneak by them. Mighty unsafe."

"No problem, I'll come in during the evening. Thanks."

Just as I'm about to hang up the phone, Margy yells over to me: "Ask about the raft at our spot."

"Oh, Jim, what about that raft at our parking spot, F-37. When we left earlier this week, it was blocking our dock."

"Oh, you're right. It's still there. I'll get it moved for you."

"Thanks. See you in a few days, if you haven't quit by then."

"Probably won't," replies Jim with a laugh.
But I bet he's thinking about it.

* * * * *

DURING OUR LAST AFTERNOON IN RICHMOND, I finish up a few routine tasks. Since I haven't yet spoken to the previous owner of the boat (we dealt with a sales broker instead), there are quite a few minor mysteries. I'll eventually talk to the owner, Fernando, over the telephone, and learn a lot about this boat from him. But for now, I can't figure out how the DVD player works in conjunction with the TV monitor. Nor have I determined how the ice chest on the swim grid got so full of water. I play with the DVD and get it working. The ice chest is a huge box mounted on the swim grid, apparently used as a fish locker, and it's nearly half full of water. So I drain the chest, still not knowing how the water got in, but I suspect it came from melted ice.

That evening, we walk to the Boat House, a local restaurant, where we eat in the pub while we watch the start of the final game of hockey's Stanley Cup on the big screen television. The pub is crowded with enthusiastic Canuck supporters, many wearing team shirts. During the first period, Boston scores quickly, calming the crowd. There's a funny feeling that's been in the air in Canada the past few days. Vancouver is on the verge of winning the Stanley Cup, with only one game left, but Boston is formidable. This morning's headlines in the *Vancouver Sun*: "Our Town, Our Team, Our Turn!" But it isn't.

It may seem to be Vancouver's (and Canada's) turn to win the Stanley Cup, after two decades of American teams stealing it right out from under the country that's the real hockey nation. Many of us, including me, have this funny feeling it's going to happen again.

What occurred during that last game in 2011 is one of those memorable international events (not of a positive kind), so important that most Canadians remember exactly where they were when the Canucks lost the last game of the Stanley Cup. In that respect, as far as Canadians are concerned, the importance of the loss ranks right up there with the Olympics. Canada is truly a hockey nation.

When we leave the restaurant after the first period of play, the place has changed from jubilant but nervous fans to an uncomfortably hushed crowd. A few miles away, at the rink where the Canucks are playing, it's the same scene.

Back at the boat, I listen to the end of the game on the radio. The score goes from bad to worse. The entire last period is agonizing, as Boston scores even more goals to pull the game entirely out of reach. When it's over, I feel bad for the Canucks, their fans, and the entire country.

As the game ends, I walk up the ramp to the marina office, to throw a bag of trash in the dumpster. While I walk back to the boat, I notice two middle-aged men and a woman slowly exiting the main dock in front of me. They're obviously coming back from a sorrowful boat party nearby, as evidenced by their blue Canucks jerseys and a downcast look.

One of the men shakes his head, and then throws an empty plastic bottle into the water next to the dock. It's a toss that's done with conscious anger. The act isn't only eco-unfriendly, it's also very un-Canadian. I watch the bottle bob up and down near the dock. It disturbs me to watch this, but I understand why the bottle has ended up in the water tonight.

* * * * *

THE NEXT MORNING, we're underway in the early morning light, a few minutes after 5 o'clock, with high tide scheduled for 5:21. The wind is calm, and the water in the marina is motionless. The sun is already up, it's low angle casting vibrant yellow rays through the clear sky.

Motoring out of the marina is relatively uneventful. At least we don't hit anything. I'm still struggling with the twin-engine shift procedures for turning the boat without touching the wheel. Once we're headed up the river towards the first bridge, everything settles down quickly. The GPS map shows a clear path out the Fraser's north arm, where the previous owner has left his old tracks in the database for me to follow (overlaid by our futile attempt to dump our holding tank). On the right side of the display, I can clearly see my recent looping track to the spot where the windlass came apart during the anchor's unscheduled freefall.

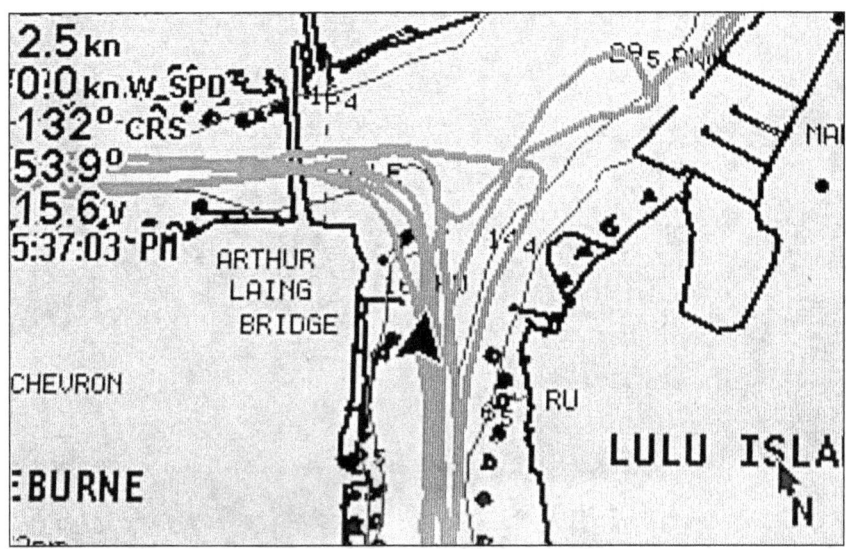

GPS view – departing Richmond

I've become familiar with these bridges. They feel like old friends. We pass under the first swinging bridge with its low clearance that makes me cringe. I hold my breath, but our tall VHF antennas don't scrape, as I know they won't.

Now it's a left turn, and then under the bigger bridge that reminds me we're really underway, headed north towards home. The early morning workday traffic is already rumbling across the bridge overhead. The sun is climbing higher – mid-June in Canada at 5:30 in the morning, only a few days until the longest day of the year.

From here, the route is simple. Margy drives while I kick back and enjoy the early morning sunlight. We're headed out the narrow north arm of the Fraser, and there's no other traffic. We expect tugs and logging booms, but even these are absent this morning.

With no traffic in sight, I take the helm, and we're ready to go up onto plane for the first time by ourselves. This is also the first time we've tried throttling up from the command bridge since the ill-fated experience with Geoff during the sea trial. I'm convinced we simply had too much weight on the upper deck that day, but now we're going to find out.

Approaching the bridge early in the morning

"Let me know if you see, feel, or hear anything unusual," I tell Margy. "I'll come back on the throttles right away if it doesn't feel right for any reason."

"Okay, I'm ready," she replies.

Conditions are perfect, so this should work. I push the throttles forward very gradually, then a bit more forcefully when all seems stable at about 10 knots. The engines pour out their loud power, and suddenly *Bang!*

It's a terrifyingly loud booming noise. Something major has happened, but what could it be? I throttle back immediately, and the bow slides back down into the water.

"What was that?!" I yell to Margy, who is looking back down at the aft deck.

"The ice chest," she calmly states. "It flew into the dinghy."

That would do it – loud and resounding, when a big ice chest whacks into an inflatable dinghy with a wooden floor.

"So that's why Fernando kept water in the ice chest," I say. "Needs the weight."

"Makes sense," replies Margy.

I climb down off the command bridge, and pull the big but lightweight, empty ice chest back onto the aft deck where it will be safe. Live and learn – the hard way. Once I see nothing has been damaged, it's worth a big laugh.

After this, going up onto plane is simple and straightforward. We're quickly cruising through smooth water at 21 knots and 3700 RPM, stable and very comfortable.

Near the end of the north arm, we pass the last barges tied along the shoreline, full of pulp and probably scheduled to go up the Fraser River to Vancouver. But it's possible they're headed in the opposite direction – north through the Strait of Georgia, maybe even destined for Powell River's own paper mill.

Ahead of us, the last stretch of the well-marked outlet displays a line of small wind waves, merely ripples on the previously flat water. Coward's Cove passes to our right, a spot where sailboats sometimes anchor to await improved conditions before venturing out into open water. Winds, waves, and tides change here, even under the best of conditions. Today it's hardly noticeable. We continue out into the

Exiting the north arm of the Fraser

ocean, soon deep enough to turn right on a direct course towards Bowen Island.

The water remains nearly flat, making our ride on-plane comfortable. But in a few more miles, the small wind waves change to noticeable swells that get bigger as we progress toward Bowen. When I turn slightly to the left towards Gibsons, the swells are big enough that I decide to drop down off the step and continue at a slower speed. I establish a GPS groundspeed of 9 knots, and it feels stable. The waves are large enough that *Halcyon Days* would have been uncomfortable here. But this boat is a lot wider, as well as longer, and handles bigger waves with ease. We'll still face days when it's too uncomfortable to travel, but it's a noticeable improvement today. No waves break over the bow, nor do I feel any spray on the command bridge. This boat will serve us well.

We continue past Gibsons, plowing water and easing in closer to shore, seeking smoother seas so we can go back up onto plane. Finally we find these conditions near Sechelt, and soon we're cruising again at over 20 knots. Margy is driving now, and she handles the boat confidently. I'm glad she seems comfortable at the helm. We cruise

Wayne on the command bridge

past Merry Island, Smuggler's Cove, and aim at the entrance to Secret Cove.

We're the first boat into the fuel dock at Secret Cove this morning. I maneuver in slowly and efficiently, as two women stand on the dock, waiting to assist with our lines. Of course, there's no wind at all, but it's nice to make such a controlled arrival. The two young women grab our docking lines and pull us tight against the rail.

Secret Cove

"Where are you from?" asks one of the women.

"Powell River," I answer. "But we came from Vancouver this morning."

"Oh! It must have been terrible there last night," she replies. "The riots and all."

"Riots? What riots?"

Then she explains what happened in downtown Vancouver after the hockey game. To listen to her description, it sounds like the entire city was on fire. To me, it was a big deal to see a guy throw a water bottle into the harbour, and I didn't even know about the rest.

After we refuel, I place the ice chest back into its swim grid mounts, using the dockside water hose to fill it a-third-full.

In the on-dock marine store, we buy hot coffee, with lids to get us to the other side of the cove where we plan to anchor for a short stay. We need the practice with our windlass, and we're way ahead of schedule. It's only 9 am, and we're halfway home, with the new marina in Powell River closed until 5 o'clock in the evening.

Our anchoring exercise is less than successful. The windlass operates fine, but several test drops result in the chain clogging the narrow entry to the anchor locker while retrieving the anchor. I go down to the V-berth to spread the chain out. It's slow process, but a minor redesign in the locker should reduce the congestion of the sliding links. I'll try installing a plastic sheet to reduce friction when I get the opportunity, but not today.

With the anchor on the bottom of the cove and extra rode extended, I settle in with my coffee, now almost cold. Still, it tastes good, the morning is spectacular, and we're on our way home. I use this break to phone Jim.

"Will I be able to come into the harbour today?"

"After 5 o'clock will work fine. Right now there's a barge blocking the entrance."

"Sounds great. What about the raft attached to the end of F-dock?"

"Let me look," Jim says, as he pauses to walk out onto his office deck.

"No, it's still there. I'll ask them to move it."

That's somewhat reassuring, since I know the situation. There's no doubt Jim will "ask," but that's pretty much the limit of his control over the situation.

"Thanks, Jim. One more thing – the moorage bill from city hall said we should check with you for access to the gangways."

When I saw this in the invoice, I assumed that no keys during payment of the moorage bill meant we're getting a gate code system or a similar high-tech secure entry. That would be quite a step up for Powell River.

"No reason to worry about getting through the gate," replies Jim with a hesitating hint of embarrassment.

"Oh, okay."

Now I get it. There'll be no problem getting through the gate because there's still no gate. The new harbour is ready, in the general sense of things, but not even close in the details.

As I finish up talking to Jim, I notice we've drifting precariously close to shore. Margy is waving at me to finish up the call quickly, and it's obvious why. Either the anchor has been dragging or there's something about anchoring this boat that I don't understand. Maybe I've lowered too much chain, and we're merely swinging wider than expected.

When I put the phone down, I hustle up to the command bridge, and start the engines. Margy takes over from me while I scoot back down and around the catwalk to the bow. Margy backs us away from shore while I lean over the bow, watching the chain pointed straight down. With this much weight, as opposed to rope, the angle of the chain appears vertical.

All ends well. Once we're in deeper water, we use the windlass to pull up the anchor, and we're successfully underway again.

The rest of the trip is through nearly calm water. We wind along the shore past familiar landmarks – Pender Harbour, Scotch Fir Point, Lang Bay, Myrtle Rocks, and around Grief Point. The Comox ferry is just pulling out of its berth when we turn into the fuel dock at the South Harbour to top off our tanks. In the calm water, I make another well-controlled arrival. Shift left, shift right, shift again and again, and our fenders bump lightly against the dock.

After refueling, we motor around the breakwater to the entrance to the North Harbour where the big crane is swinging concrete docks into position. A sign on the breakwater says: "Harbour Closed for Maintenance." A one-liner below the notice lists the phone number to call for further information. Of course, it's Jim's phone number. His phone rings a lot these days.

We float here for a few minutes, watching the big crane swing. Then we go a few hundred metres farther north along the shore to Willingdon Beach, where we make a flawless anchor drop in 40 feet of water.

We spend a leisurely afternoon swinging on anchor in the light breeze. High-school-age kids sit on the Willingdon dock, feet splashing the water. School is out for the summer, and this is the way life should be for both them and us.

As 5 o'clock approaches, we watch the crane and its barge moving towards shore. A few minutes after 5:00, we weigh anchor and ease our way into the harbour. All is quiet.

Powell River's North Harbour entrance blocked by crane

Not only is it quiet, it's exceptionally quiet. Only a few boats occupy the marina, with most slips vacant. Jim has given me more than I expected – an approved arrival ahead of most of the rest of the marina's occupants. I'm grateful.

Empty North Harbour

But our assigned spot on the end of F-dock is still occupied by the raft that obstructs our parking. In other words, I conclude, Jim struck out when he tried to get it moved. That's not unexpected, and there's plenty of parking elsewhere tonight, so I slide into a drift-in spot near where I'm supposed to park. My arrival is nearly flawless for a new twin-engine driver. We're home!

Chapter 8

Zincs and Wheelbarrows

The morning after the arrival of the Bayliner 3058 in Powell River's North Harbour, I see Margy off on Pacific Coastal, and hang around town waiting for John to get off work from a painting job south of town. Our plan is to go out on a local ride in the new Bayliner after 5 o'clock to introduce John to the boat. By then, the harbour will be open again. But clouds move in, and a bit of wind comes up, without any significant change in sea conditions. When weather changes in Powell River, it can happen dramatically, and this has the precursor feeling of such conditions.

John calls soon after 6 o'clock, saying he's really tired and is concerned about the rising wind relative to even a local trip on the chuck. As is often the case, his remarks are second-hand through Margy's cell phone, since she's now in Bellingham. Her Canadian phone number is the most economical way for John to contact me, although internationally indirect.

When Margy relays the message, I laugh.

"You know, if I didn't know better, I'd think John is just a little hesitant about learning to drive a twin-engine boat. When we discussed tonight's trip, he even said it might be best if I maneuvered the boat out of the harbour."

"John is going to let you drive?" says Margy.

"I know it's hard to believe. He always drives when we're together."

An hour later, I realize John is right once again. The chuck is beginning to howl.

* * * * *

REGARDLESS OF THE WIND, I go down to the marina, and prepare to move the boat two slips away to our assigned spot. The construction raft is finally gone, and I'll be able to reposition the boat to my assigned slip. In gusty winds, I start the engines, and begin to unhook the lines. Immediately, the bow swings away from the dock, and it's a frantic leap onto the aft deck to avoid watching the boat depart without me.

I rush up to the command bridge, and struggle for control of the swinging vessel, finally executing a looping departure without hitting anything. Once positioned in the waterway between the dock fingers, I stagger out towards the breakwater, planning to turn 180 degrees back towards my assigned spot along the main waterway. There's plenty of space here, but now the quickly escalating wind is pushing me towards the breakwater. Shift-shift-shift-throttle-throttle! Somehow I manage a 90-degree turn to prevent disaster, and I get the boat pointed out of the main channel towards the marina entrance. My revised plan (if you can call it that) is to turn around in the wide area near the crane, and head back towards my slip in a more organized fashion.

On my first try, I turn the boat around in the wide area near the entrance, and head back to my slip. But I'm blown away from my mooring spot when I try to come in close to the dock. So I repeat the sequence – turn around, and then back out to the entrance for a 180 course reversal, and then back to the dock, only to be blown away from it again – three more times! In the strong opposing wind, I can't get close enough to the dock to hop off.

I try everything I can think of, including one engine in neutral while the other is used to maneuver, hoping my single-engine experience will override the conditions. Finally, on my fifth approach, help arrives. I see a man and a woman running down the dock finger to my rescue.

"We saw you from way over there, when we were parking our boat," the man yells up to me on the command bridge as I come in close once again. "Looked like you were in trouble."

"You bet I am," I respond, while maneuvering close to the slip, where I can hover fairly easy, but never quite close enough to jump off onto the dock. (In fact, when it's all over, I review the situation in my mind. After a few balked tries, I considered getting as close as possible to the dock, where I could then jump ashore with the stern line. Imagine the force it would take to haul a 30-foot boat up to the dock in a strong opposing wind with a single line. It's a good thing I never got close enough to jump out.)

"Try aiming at me," the man suggests. "Just bow it in, and I'll grab you."

It works! While the man holds the bow rail tight, I throw my stern line to the woman. She quickly wraps it around a cleat, slowly hauls me in, and I'm finally safe.

"We saw you going round and round," relates the woman. "It took us awhile to get here. We were on our boat on a finger at the other end of the harbour, and had to run all the way to shore and then down to your gangway. Must have taken us ten minutes."

"Seemed like a lifetime," I laugh.

But I'm really home now – parked in my own slip in the new North Harbour.

* * * * *

THE NEXT MORNING, a Saturday, I've scheduled a unique solution to in-water boat maintenance. Many tasks require hauling a boat out of the water, and that isn't easy with a 30-footer, especially considering the current state of the new (almost finished) harbour. The launch ramp is barely operational, with no adjacent dock yet constructed. And local boat shops are in a tizzy, with scheduled launches and boat maintenance backing up from a nine-month period of harbour construction. Getting an appointment with a local shop for haul-out is out of the question.

Yet I have a maintenance item that needs immediate attention. Back in Richmond, during the marine survey haul-out in the sling, several of the stern zincs were identified as needing replacement soon. Over time, these important sacrificial chunks of metal corrode away when placed in contact with salt water. Mounted on stern-drives and other steel components (such as trim tabs), they are eaten away intentionally so the steel remains unaffected. Zincs are critical components of the transom. And my zincs have been identified as needing almost immediate attention.

But when the Bayliner was hauled-out for the marine survey, the sling crane was available for only an hour, the minimum time required for the inspection. There was no time to change the deteriorated zincs. While the boat remained in the semi-saline water of the lower Fraser River, this wasn't of major concern.

Now that we're docked in the North Harbour's salty water, replacement of the zincs is required right away. It's a simple process, once the boat is out of the water, but getting it hauled out under the current circumstances is nearly impossible. Margy comes up with an idea, which I later learn is common among those who own big boats.

"What about a diver?" she asks. "Couldn't someone go down to change the zincs right in the harbour?"

It seems like a possibility, and a phone call to Powell River Divers provides a solution.

"How about Saturday morning?" says Ken. "I can send Roger over at 10 o'clock to take care of the zincs."

How timely! Maybe it makes a difference that Ken dove under my cabin to replace flotation barrels, and maybe it's just because getting things done in Powell River is often amazingly simple.

On Saturday morning, John shows up at the dock first, helping me with another project – getting the dinghy's outboard motor running. It's the first test of the dinghy and engine, and I'm soon convinced this big, ugly inflatable may be worth keeping. (A coat of paint will soon

John and Bro checkout the dinghy

make it look like new.) Once removed from the swim grid, we leave the small boat floating nearby, so it will be out of the diver's way.

When Roger shows up, I'm quickly impressed. He's an obvious expert diver, and a very interesting fellow. When he suggests we move the boat closer to the gangway for easier access to his truck full of tools and diving equipment, I'm hesitant about moving the boat.

"I'm not very confident about moving into a congested area," I say. "I'm new to this boat, and so is John."

"Can I help?" he asks. "I'll even drive, if you prefer."

Would I ever prefer it that way! As it turns out, Roger is an experienced crew boat captain. I take him up on his offer to move the boat, and he gives me valuable twin-engine maneuvering instructions on the way over to the gangway.

"The biggest problem most people encounter when they're new to twin screws is going too fast and using the wheel too much," he advises. "Just take it real slow, and let the momentum of the boat do all of the work."

Roger changing the zincs

I watch in awe as he slides expertly into the slip nearest to the gangway. Shift-shift-shift – our slow momentum bumps us softly against the dock with unhurried precision.

The rest of today's operation draws the attention of those walking down the gangway. Roger patiently stops his work now-and-then to explain what he's doing to interested people who pass by, including a family with two small children who are fascinated by Roger in his dry suit and tank.

With the boat securely back in its slip, and new zincs in place, I work on some onboard tasks – reorganizing equipment and cleaning up the boat's cabin. Add to that some extensive kick-back-and-relax time – reading in the sun and even a nap in the V-berth – and the day is soon over. By the time I'm finished, the sun has set, but there's still one more task I'd like to complete today.

I want to swap the boat's huge microwave oven with a smaller model currently in the condo. This will provide more free space in the boat and a bigger microwave for the condo. So in what remains of the mid-June twilight, I walk up to the condo, and load the small microwave into my truck. I park in Marine Traders parking lot, and lug the microwave to the marina. A wooden wheelbarrow sits at the gangway entry, which makes the rest of the trip to the boat a lot easier.

After swapping the microwaves, I use the wheelbarrow for the trip back to the truck. By now it's 11:00, and quite dark. After exiting the gangway, I push the wheelbarrow around piles of dirt at the entrance to the new marina, headed for my truck. I weave around red cones and a big bulldozer. Walking down the dirt road in the opposite direction is a man and his dog.

"I bet this looks rather suspicious, doesn't it?" I say to the man. "Pushing a big microwave in a wheelbarrow out of the marina this time of night."

"I didn't see a thing," he says. "Do you know where I can find out where I'm supposed to park my boat? They sent me a notice in the mail with my new parking spot, but I threw it away."

I'm unable to help a local who throws his mail in the trash, although the same man is perfectly willing to let a guy with a suspicious microwave pass by without question. I continue past the dirt piles and across the ferry access lane where a line of cars awaits the last Texada Island trip of the day. People look up from their books and magazines, as if they consider a man pushing a wheelbarrow containing a large microwave oven standard procedure this time of night.

The big microwave makes it to the condo, and the comparatively "tiny" microwave now sits safely in the boat. It's been a very full day, and I'm pleasantly exhausted by the tasks that have been completed, zincs and wheelbarrows included.

Chapter 9

Downrigger Rookie

On Powell Lake, I finally upgrade my tin boat. During the winter, I pull the boat onto the float cabin's upper deck, flip it over, and clean around all the rivets with a wire brush. Then I apply the solder-like repair material that forms the basis of a repair kit for aluminum boats. Using a propane torch, I heat the rivets and melt the synthetic "solder" in green globs.

John is suspicious: "Too simple," he notes. "Can't work, at least not for long."

What he says sounds valid. Yet, the sealed areas seem tough. After a full week of working with the rivets, I launch the boat, and the floor stays dry. But how long will it last?

Two years later, I'm still asking how such a simple repair can be so permanent. But, so far, it's a lasting solution. Even with constant abuse to the lower hull by scraping on gravel beaches and the cabin's dock as I pull the tin boat out of the water, the repairs hold. Over time, aluminum boats (except welded non-rivet style boats) always leak. But finally I have a tin boat with minimum seeps. Which is enough to entice me into further upgrades.

I add a fishfinder, and then a small manual downrigger. I troll along the relatively-deep water near the shore with a cannonball dropped 20 feet down, and watch the fishfinder to assure I don't get hung up on the bottom. Operating the small outboard while monitoring my fishing rod and the downrigger takes some attention, and occasionally I hook a log or boulder. But I make it through the entire spring fishing season without losing a lure or a cannonball. And I even catch a few trout that might have been missed by my old-fashioned shallow trolling without a downrigger. It's a fun way to fish, and I deem it a big success.

Tin boat with downrigger and ṬshṬnder

After a little experience with the manual outrigger, I'm ready to try saltwater fishing with professional equipment. I've been fishing in the chuck for 10 years, and everybody seems to have a downrigger except me. It feels like a big step forward.

* * * * *

WHEN I PURCHASE THE BAYLINER 2452 IN BELLINGHAM, it comes with two electric downriggers. The aft gunwale mounts and electrical receptacles are of hefty Penn design. One downrigger is enough for this boat, and the other can be taken to Canada for use on the new Bayliner. Of course, this will require some modifications.

First, the Bayliner 3058 has Scotty mounts on the stern, with compatible electrical receptacles. The Penn downrigger isn't compatible with the Scotty design, so that means a lot of engineering for a guy like me. Especially when you do everything at least twice.

To remove the mount on the Bellingham boat, I ask Jeanne to assist me. While I lay on the aft deck, trying to reach the mount bolts through a small access panel, she holds the bolt heads with the appropriate screwdriver. It's a twisted struggle, but together we make it to the last bolt when some unexpected visitors show up.

"Are you taking on water?" asks a concerned man, accompanied by his friend.

"What?" is my confused reply, still contorted under the gunnel.

"We've been watching from the other dock," notes the man. "Your transom is leaning severely to the port side."

"Oh," I reply. "We're just trying to get some bolts out. I guess we're pulling the stern down pretty low."

I glance over the transom at the swim ladder, which is totally submerged on the side we're working. I can see how a passer-by would think we're sinking.

"Sorry, didn't mean to bother you," replies the man.

"No problem. I appreciate your concern."

As we wrestle with the last bolt, it's a good laugh for Jeanne and me. We may be struggling, but at least we're not sinking.

* * * * *

Back in Powell River, the modification progresses slowly. I replace the Scotty mount with its Penn counterpart that I've brought from Bellingham. This requires more contortions, reaching up through an access panel to grasp the lock nuts while keeping another hand on the screwdriver above the mount location. But with some help from Margy, I finally get the mount where I want it.

Then I tackle the electrical receptacle, which is similarly positioned in a difficult-to-access spot. I struggle with removal of the old receptacle, drill a larger hole for the new wiring harness, mount the new connector, and attach it to the downrigger.

No sooner do I finish this project than I decide to turn the boat around in its slip. The new mooring arrangement allows starboard docking, which is a better choice for my on-board equipment and provides easy get-going departures from the dock. But now I'll need to trip over the downrigger to get aboard. The solution is obvious, but not pleasant – move the mount and receptacle to the other side of the stern. This repeat installation goes quicker than the first, as is common with such tasks. Still, it means some more unnatural bending of my body before I'm finally ready to fish. Do it twice (the first time for practice) seems to be my motto.

* * * * *

MY FIRST SOLO OVERNIGHT ANCHORAGE in *Foghorn* is at Van Anda, where I tuck into the scenic bay just north of the marina. (Yes, this boat did come with an official name, *Foghorn*, but I seldom use it when referring to this Bayliner. Since I seldom use the horn, and never navigate on the ocean during fog, the name seems inappropriate.)

The next morning is ideal for testing my new downrigger – nearly calm conditions and lots of time to spare on my way back to Powell River. I plan to troll towards Texada's Blubber Bay, leisurely working my way along the relatively deep water of the coastline.

Unlike my tin boat, there's no way to drive this vessel while remaining within easy reach of the downrigger. From the command bridge, the route to the stern includes four steps down to the main deck. The lower helm isn't any closer.

Downrigger with cannonball

I prefer to be moving forward when I lower the cannonball, today attached to a day-glow green flasher and its lure, a runny-nose hoochie. So to keep things under control (relatively), I move slowly forward with both engines idling, but only one in gear. I point the nose away from the shoreline, to assure I have plenty of time to get the cannonball down and my fishing rig organized.

While I attend to the downrigger, the boat turns in a wide circle, but I'm far enough from shore to feel comfortable with the situation. When I've finished lowering the cannonball to a depth of 80 feet, I climb back up to the command bridge, and settle down on a course that brings me back towards Texada Island.

I intercept the 150-foot contour line on the GPS, and follow it north along the shoreline. The fishfinder provides backup data regarding depth, along with the reassuring (but typically unreliable) beeping of fish icons. This is going to work just fine!

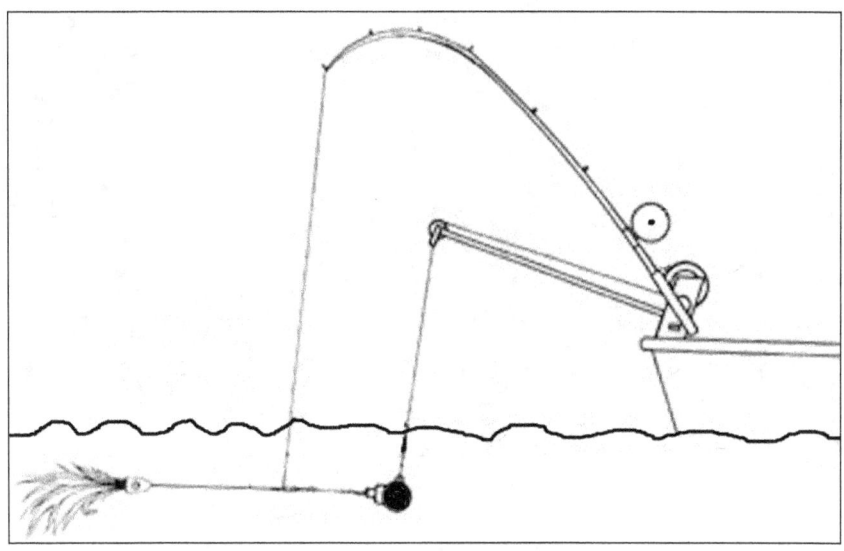

Downrigger setup

With my fishing rod positioned in the rod holder, the pole bends sharply backward, verifying that the line clip is still attached to the cannonball. Some rocks appear off the bow, extending outward far enough that I decide to navigate to the starboard side, out into deeper water for now. Additionally, the GPS depicts a reef extending a short distance beyond the rocks. I'll need to steer clear of that shallow spot, too.

From the command bridge, I stretch my neck backward, watching my fishing pole out of the corner of my eye. The pole continues to bend rearward as I would expect prior to hooking a fish. When using a downrigger, the rod stays bent until a fish strikes. Then, when the fish pulls the line clip loose from the cannonball, the slack causes the pole to momentarily straighten. So I'm waiting for that magic moment. But more important is the subtle success of this first test of my oceanic downrigger.

Downrigger in action

A small boat has appeared in the distance, nearly straight ahead. At first, it looks like a kayak, but it quickly grows to a runabout with a big tube stowed on its bow. This vessel is moving slowly, but straight towards me, probably trolling at the same depth, maybe following the same contour line on his GPS.

Collision isn't imminent, but somebody has to give way. We both have fishing lines out, and I want to avoid entanglement. I can move to the left or the right, since the other boat seems to be trekking straight towards me. But I choose the left, which isn't the best choice.

Soon after I turn, I realize my mistake. I'm wedging myself between the small boat and the reef, but now the other boat has eased outward, which cements my decision. The digital depthsounder shows 100 feet, and my cannonball is down only 80 feet. In what seems like an instant, the digital display registers 70, which means the ball is bouncing off the bottom.

Yet I can't leave the command bridge to attend to the downrigger now. The shore is too close on my left side, and the other boat is passing on the right. So I shift into neutral, waiting for the runabout to clear the area. The depthsounder stops at 50 feet, plenty of water for this boat, but not nearly enough for my cannonball, flasher, and lure. And there's forward momentum to consider. I'll slip into even shallower water on this heading, and reverse thrust isn't a good option. My fishing line is now floundering behind the Bayliner, where it can wrap itself around the prop or be cut. So I wait, drifting to a stop in 40-feet of water.

Looking back and down at the aft deck, I can see my fishing pole is no longer bent. Either I've hooked a fish (unlikely), or my lure has already caught on the bottom, maybe with the line already broken (more likely). And what about the cannonball? Is it still dragging bottom, or is it gone?

As the runabout passes, I climb down to check the downrigger. What I find can be best described in one word – "Gone." My lure and flasher are gone, and so is the cannonball.

So far, I've been fishing about a half-hour with my recently-installed electric downrigger. It didn't take long to lose my entire setup. But there are other runny-nose hoochies, other flashers, and lots of cannonballs on store shelves. So I do the only practical thing I can think of – I laugh at myself until my ribs ache. Then I climb back up onto the command bridge, and settle in for the ride home.

Chapter 10

First Trip North

Margy and I prepare for our first cruise into the northern portion of the Strait of Georgia in the new Bayliner. We pack a chicken dinner, and walk down to the boat from our condo. The nice thing about having our boat nearby is how easy it is to get up and go. This is our first experience with shore power, and it's a luxury to find drinks already cold in the refrigerator and hot water awaiting us from in faucet.

On this warm afternoon in July, with the wind light from the northwest, we motor out of the harbour with no firm destination in mind except "North." I maneuver confidently from the command bridge – out of the breakwater entrance and towards Willingdon Beach, where I turn the helm over to Margy. While still at nearly idle power, I rig up my fishing pole for trolling along the shore, which will take us past the Hulks and the paper mill, where other fishermen have caught numerous salmon recently. It's an unusual way to begin a trip, but I want to try out the downrigger again, to assure myself that I can get at least as far as the paper mill without losing the entire setup again.

While Margy drives, I have all the time in the world to set up the downrigger for trolling. It's a big improvement over my harried first-troll along Texada's shoreline.

The cannonball drops flawlessly. The fishing pole is bent over with the proper tension, with its flasher and cop-car lure traveling smoothly at a depth of 80 feet.

After assuring all is well with the downrigger and pole, I climb back up to the command bridge to join Margy until the first fish hits the lure. Always optimistic! Then I'll be ready to climb back downstairs quickly to haul in the catch. It's amazing how relaxed this system is from my frantic solo efforts. A fisherman with a separate boat operator makes all the difference.

Margy drives with the starboard engine near idle and the port engine shutdown. That's plenty of power for trolling, and the wide gap between us and the shoreline provides an adequate safety margin if we need to crank up the other engine. The result is a pleasant slow troll at 2 knots. We encounter no fish, but enjoy our leisurely slow-cruise along the shore.

Margy trolling past the Hulks near the paper mill

After passing the shallow area at the mouth of Powell River, where the water flows out into the ocean just north of the mill, I retrieve my cannonball and lure, and we're quickly up onto plane, headed towards Lund. I'm driving now, but ready to turn things over to Margy again for another slow troll past the cliffs near the Iron Mines south of Lund.

"Are you sure the fuel dock doesn't close early?" asks Margy, as we pass the big floating buoy called Atrevida Marker.

"I wouldn't think so," I reply. "Afterall, it's summer."

We both laugh, since nothing is for sure in this part of the boating world. Maybe a stop at the Iron Mines will get us to the gas dock too late. So we decide to press on nonstop to Lund, just in case. We can troll along the Mines tomorrow during our trip back south.

* * * * *

I'M A BIT APPREHENSIVE about my approach to Lund's fuel dock, since I'm still new to this boat, and this can be a busy place during the summer. But all works out remarkably well. The fueling area is vacant on the south side, and water is washing up against the dock from that direction, pushing us against the railing nicely during our arrival. We're quickly stopped, and our port lines secured. You'd hardly know I was new at this twin-engine thing.

As I begin pumping our gas, a big sailboat bears down on us. It seems this huge boat is coming in too fast, but the captain provides a fine display of maneuvering by halting about 10 metres behind us. However, after the boat is stopped, the fuel attendant helps the captain pull the sailboat farther forward, right up to our stern, and then secures the lines tight.

"Good to have an inflatable back there, eh?" I say to Margy.

She laughs, but it does seem strange the sailboat would pull up so close on purpose. Maybe the boat's fuel tank position relative to

The sailboat behind our dinghy

the dock was part of the decision. In any case, I finish pumping our gasoline, while the expensive-looking sailboat takes on diesel fuel.

During our short stay at the fueling area, the waves pick up noticeably, now pounding the dock pretty strong. For Lund, this isn't unusual. I've seen major wave action here in the past, no doubt attributable to the geography of the harbour and the placement of the fuel dock. When you add to this the nearly-constant wake of often-too-fast Savary water taxis, Lund can be an exciting experience. Which is how it turns out today.

"This place always gets worse after you arrive," I comment to Margy.

"I'll be glad when we're gone," she replies.

I can tell she's nervous about the increasing waves and the big sailboat behind us. Which should be a warning indicator to me, but I often fail to look before I leap.

The fuel attendant helps us unfasten our lines, and pushes our stern outward. At first, it seems like plenty of clearance from the shiny million-dollar-looking sailboat, so I shift into reverse on the port engine (simultaneously forward on the starboard), and our Bayliner starts easing away from the dock. I can't help thinking this sailboat costs at least ten times the price of our Bayliner, with not much more "crap" than we have. I remember the words of Dick in LaConner: "Lots of people call Bayliners crappy boats, but you sure get a lot of crap for your money."

But boats, including Bayliners, don't always maneuver in reverse very well, which is why boaters often speak of how their boat "walks" in reverse. In today's case, it's more of a hobbled trot. Although my port engine is in reverse and my starboard engine in forward (which, in theory, should push our stern promptly outward from the dock), the Bayliner is "walking" slower than the incoming waves. As a result, we're now moving parallel to the dock rather than away from it, and back towards the big-buck sailboat.

The captain's first mate (a blond woman with a look of fear on her face) runs along the outboard rail of the sailboat, thrusting a big rubber fender towards us as a shield. She's prepared to prevent a collision by dropping the fender wherever it looks like we might land on her vessel. I'm sure she sees the word "Bayliner" on the side of our boat, and I bet she's thinking about how "crappy" such a boat is compared to hers.

Fortunately, I catch the situation in time, throttling up on both engines to take our stern outward from the sailboat. Then I begin backing away from the dock, now well clear. The sailboat captain, fuel attendant, and first mate are all watching me intently, so I wave: "Bye now."

"Just keep going backward!" yells the captain, partly in an attempt to offer encouragement, and partly to get his two cents in. (In other words: "Get that crappy boat out of here!")

"Did you see the look on her face?" I ask Margy when we're finally clear and underway again.

"Sure did. It was intense. She certainly had a firm grip on that big fender."

"Didn't want to get hit by a Bayliner, did she?"

* * * * *

ALL SETTLES DOWN QUICKLY, and we laugh our way up onto plane.

"How about Cortes Bay?" I ask.

"Sounds good," replies Margy.

It's that simple for us. We sometimes don't decide where we're going until we're well underway. And that's part of the fun.

Cortes Bay is one of our favourite places, and less than an hour to the north. The sea is cooperating, with the lightest of chop, and soon we're pulling through the entrance, keeping the red marker and the barely-submerged reef off our right side. Inside the harbour, all of the large dock spaces (which we need) are occupied, but we're planning on anchoring tonight anyway. There's plenty of open area between the government dock and the Seattle Yacht Club to the south (the Vancouver Yacht Club has an equally large facility to the north). Several sailboats are on mooring balls, and we position ourselves to anchor in slightly deeper water, but still adequate for dropping a hook in this sheltered bay.

With a depth of 40 feet, we use all of our chain (92 feet) and are well into 30 feet of our rope, for a scope of 3-to-1. That should be more than enough for this protected location, but right away we appear to be dragging anchor in a very light wind. So I go back to the bow, raise the anchor enough to clear the bottom, and Margy drives us forward and into position again. This time, dropping in nearly the same location, the anchor catches adequately, and we're firmly hooked. Sometimes anchoring is like that – not all can be explained, so you just need to play with it until it works.

Cortes Bay sunset

Soon after we've settled in, an impressive "mothership" arrives and drops anchor in slightly deeper water near the harbour's entrance. It really does look like a mothership, and even acts like one. In just a few minutes, two Bayliner Trophies have pulled up to the 150-foot (estimated) powerboat, and their occupants climb aboard the mothership. A few minutes later, one of the Trophies departs, but the other stays moored to the big boat all night. In my mind, I visualize the mothership dropping off kayakers in Desolation Sound, and then returning to port to pick them up on another day. Of course, I don't know this is so, but it satisfies my imagination.

Being around boats creates its own excitement, often involving how small the regional boating community seems to be. You see boats you've never seen before, and you see boats you recognize. One of the never-before-seen fishing boats pulls into the harbour just before sunset, a classic vessel like many plying these waters. It rafts up to another boat at the nearby government dock, and the fishermen talk and laugh well into the evening. Sound travels well over water. We can't hear what they're saying, but they're certainly having a good time.

Another boat exits the harbour just before dark. This boat we recognize.

"That's the Coast Guard rubber boat that rescued us in Okeover," says Margy.

Sure enough, it's the twin-outboard Hurricane Zodiac that assisted us when we suffered engine problems in our old Bayliner (*Farther Up the Strait*, Chapter 5). At the time, the inflatable boat came to our rescue from the Comox Coast Guard's summer base in Cortes Bay. Here they are again, probably going out on a routine training mission. The sight of this boat reminds us of an overly exciting day that eventually morphed into a fond memory of meeting the Coast Guard up close and personal.

We finish our evening with a chicken dinner, and then lounge around the boat in a satisfied sense of relaxation. I climb up onto the command bridge, stretch out, and read. Meanwhile, Margy finds a

Margy on the aft deck

comfortable spot on the aft deck, playing a computer game on her iPad. As expected, this is another perfect spot to enjoy the sport of overnight anchoring.

* * * * *

The next morning dawns quiet in peaceful Cortes Bay. We leisurely prepare for departure. Margy operates the remote-controlled windlass from the command bridge, while I go out to the bow to supervise the retrieval. When the anchor is secure, I signal to Margy, waving my arm towards the bay's entrance. She slowly navigates out of the harbour. When I join her on the command bridge, she asks me to take over while we go up onto plane for the trip home and our planned trolling segment near the Iron Mines just south of Lund.

When I add power on the engines, all is normal, and we come up onto plane as expected. Then, suddenly, the RPM of the port engine falls off. I watch the tachometer drop through 2000 before I finally pull back on both throttles until they're at idle.

Could we have picked up some seaweed that's affected the prop? It's a fairly common occurrence, easily solved by reversing the engines briefly, then coming back up onto plane.

But this time, it's not the solution. When I power up again, both engines wind up to 3600 RPM, but then the port engine drops off again, this time completely shutting down on its own.

I restart the engine, shift into gear again, and try adding power on both engines. As long as I remain below 3000 RPM, all is well. But at throttle settings needed to stay on plane, the power of the port motor immediately drops off. Both engines sound flawless at lower throttle settings. I work with it over and over again, before I finally resolve we're going to be going home at trawler speed.

We trudge back home, pushing water at 9 knots. In this particular hull, designed for faster speeds, it's not a fuel-efficient situation. But there's no choice today. We forego our plans for fishing along the Iron Mines, and do our best to enjoy the slow trip south. And in fact, it's enjoyable to us. Sure, it's not fun to experience an engine problem. But it must be something simple, since the engine runs so well at low RPMs, and it's nice weather for just slogging along. We don't have far to go, so it's no big deal.

"Maybe we picked up a fishing line in our prop," suggests Margy.

"Maybe, but it doesn't fit with how well the engine runs at slow speeds," I reply.

Even when I've tested the engine at high RPMs in neutral, the engine purrs smoothly. Only under load at high RPMs does anything unusual occur.

Once back in our berth in the North Harbour, I raise the stern legs to visually check the props. There's still the possibility we've picked up a fishing line. What I find is a bit of a surprise.

There's no entangled line, but the port engine (which happens to be the affected motor) is missing its zinc fin. This small anti-corrosion tab normally rests right above the prop, and it's one of the zinc elements recently replaced when the scuba diver swapped out my old zincs. The diver had difficulties with this particular fin, but finally got it secured. Now it's pretty obvious it wasn't as tight as we thought, since it has fallen off. Strange coincidence – a zinc missing from the same engine that's experienced the loss of power. I think it through, and can't see any relationship that makes sense, although a missing zinc would change the water flow pattern from the propeller, but surely not enough to cause such a significant power problem.

My obvious course of action is to consult John. He'll have some ideas. And, of course, he does.

When I explain all the details, including the coincidentally missing zinc fin, he suggests starting at the distributor cap.

"It's either ignition or fuel," he says. "And the distributor is easy to check, so I'd try that first."

"What about the missing fin?" I ask.

"So what?" he replies.

Recently, in the Campion that I use for travel up and down Powell Lake, distributor connectors caked with corrosion had caused similar problems. So John's suggestion seems plausible.

The next day I pull the distributor, and check for corrosion. Yes, there's definitely a build-up of rusty spots in the distributor, which would equate to loss of power. But, as is often the case, I'm not sure if what I've found is normal or abnormal. My experience in such matters is too limited. But there's a nice thing about a twin-engine boat – you always have another engine to use as your baseline.

So after I clean up the distributor, I removed the distributor cap from the other engine, and find it almost as corroded as the bad engine. When I see the comparatively similar corrosion, I know the solution might not be as obvious as I thought. Yes, the distributor connections are a little corroded, but the interiors of the two caps don't look significantly different from each other. And only one engine has operational problems.

So I put the caps back on the engines, and take the Bayliner out for a test run, hoping that cleaning the port cap might have changed something. The problem isn't resolved – at high RPMs, the port engine still falls off in power.

When I get back to the dock, I phone John, and report the results. He has another suggestion.

"It could be fuel," he says. "A clogged filter could allow the engine to run just fine when you're idling, since you don't need much gas for that. But when you add more throttle, a contaminated filter wouldn't allow enough fuel to give you maximum power. That could be it."

At this point, we're pretty much shooting in the dark. But we are tackling the simple tasks first. We have the time and we're willing to put in the effort, so we plan to follow this through a bit further before contacting the boat repair shop. Not only is it cheaper to solve your own problems, you also learn along the way.

* * * * *

ON MY NEXT VISIT TO THE BOAT, I bring a filter wrench I purchased at Canadian Tire. I'm not much of a mechanic, but I've recently acquired an increased desire to try more things on my own before deferring to John. I need to learn, and there's nothing like attacking simple tasks along the way to make myself more proficient regarding general maintenance tasks.

After a few minutes at the boat, I return to Canadian Tire to trade the filter wrench for the next bigger size. As is often the case, my repair expertise is so minimal that I tend to do most tasks more than once – the first time is just practice.

By the end of the day, I've accomplished what John could have done in a few minutes. The fuel filter is changed, and I've even replaced the missing zinc fin – with the stern leg raised, it's accessible from the dinghy. Both tasks are more challenging than I'd expected, but at least I've been able to complete them on my own. That's an accomplishment in itself.

However, I'm not sure the fuel filer was dirty enough to cause the power loss problem. There's definitely contamination inside the filter (a small amount of water), but is it enough to cause a loss of power? A quick test run outside the harbour will answer the question.

Thus, another test run. When I try to come up onto plane, the RPM again drops back suddenly. The problem persists exactly as before.

Now distraught by what is obviously a more serious problem than originally expected, I drive back through the harbour's entrance and pull into my parking spot. At least I'm getting lots of twin-engine docking practice just going out for these test runs.

When I return to the dock, I do one more thing that will later come back to haunt me. I raise the legs of both engines high enough to check the zinc fins. In the fading light of sunset, it's tough to tell whether both fins are there, especially with the overhanging inflatable dinghy partially blocking the view. So I return to the helm and turn the wheel full-throw to the right, which gives me a better view looking from the dock towards the stern legs. Now I can clearly see that both zinc fins are still attached. If a fin could fall off after being attached by a qualified diver, I'm pleased to confirm the new fin has made it through at least one brief trip on the chuck after being fastened by me.

With nightfall coming on fast, I climb back up to the command bridge and lower both legs to their full down position. Then I pick up my loose tools and head back up the hill to call John and report my nearly wasted day.

* * * * *

"It's gotta be either fuel or ignition," reiterates John on the phone. "Do you want to go out in the boat together to see what we can find?"

The implications were two-sided: One – John wants to see the problem for himself; and Two – he's ready to step in and get busy fixing things rather than merely relaying instructions to me. One thing for sure, when he tackles a problem, he never gives up until it's fixed.

Thus, the next morning, we meet at the harbour. Before departing, John asks a strange question:

"Why don't you drive today?"

This is a very strange request. Never have I driven a boat with John aboard. It's simply protocol, and it's accepted by both of us. When John and I are aboard a boat together, he drives. After all, he's the experienced boater, and I readily accept his position as captain. It's just the way it always is, and that's fine with both of us, no matter whose boat is involved.

But today he has some doubts. With all of his boating experience, John has never driven a twin-engine vessel, and he admits to being apprehensive about it. Part of that concern is undoubtedly from what he's heard from me.

"I'm having a heck of a time with this boat," I tell him soon after purchasing the 30-foot Bayliner. "Driving it requires keeping the wheel straight ahead during docking, and using the shift levers for differential steering."

It's true, or so I've come to accept, based on what I've heard from others. They all say to keep the wheel straight, and proceed slowly at idle, using the shift levers in coordination when maneuvering near a dock. I've watched boaters do it, too, and it works well. But having driven only a single-screw boat previously, it's a whole different mindset. I'm used to "kicking the ass around" during docking, by abruptly turning the wheel, and shoving the throttle into reverse. With two engines and a little experience, a boat can be maneuvered in very tight confines. But without some experience, it can be sight to behold (meaning, very ugly).

"You should be able to drive twin engines just like a single-engine boat," says John.

He says this to challenge me (one of his favourite things). I know he's listening and absorbing what I say, but he pretends to ignore me.

"But all the experts say you need to use the shift levers, and keep the wheel pointed straight ahead when you're docking," I reply. "Maybe with lots of experience, you can use the wheel, but I don't recommend it at first."

Now there's an ironic twist of words. Am I actually telling John how to drive a boat? My guess is he could drive it like a single-engine boat, if he wanted to, and still maneuver better than me.

On the other hand, he's obviously reluctant about driving this boat. In fact, he's so reluctant he actually suggests I drive during our first departure from the dock. It's enough to make me a nervous wreck.

"Are you sure you don't want to drive?" I ask, after we have the engines running and are ready to cast off. "I'm fine with you driving, you know."

"No, no. You go ahead. I'll take over once we get outside the harbour."

He's really going to let me do this, so I'd better do it right. I make sure my red tape mark on the steering wheel is at the top, indicating the engines are properly positioned straight ahead. Then I shift into gear, and angle out away from the dock. When I begin to drift towards the rock breakwater, I apply differential shift levers – port forward, starboard in neutral, which should quickly return me to the center of the narrow waterway. But it doesn't!

In fact, I drift even closer to the rocks, as if some unforeseen underwater current is at work today. I'm closing on the breakwater so fast that I add a touch of power on the port engine, which does the trick, but a little too abruptly.

"You're too close to the rocks!" yells John, as he hustles down from the command bridge, grabs the pike pole, and stands by to defend our boat from crashing into the breakwater.

"It's okay!" I yell down to him. "We're headed back to the center again."

And we are, but the boat is now sliding sideways in the waterway, not at all under control. I shift the starboard engine into forward, trying to straighten the boat. And the Bayliner slides sideways towards the row of boats on my right!

"Stop! Stop! You're gonna' hit those boats!" screams John.

He's right – I'm headed towards the dock, but his "suggestions" aren't making things any easier.

What's going on here?! It's as if the steering wheel is full to the right. Yet the tape mark on the wheel shows me it's straight. Wait a minute!

Suddenly, it dawns on me. The wheel's tape mark is straight up, but the wheel is a full revolution to the right of center. When I raised the legs last night to check the zinc fins, I turned the wheel full right to see the legs better from the dock. I never turned the engines back to straight.

In an instant, all is solved. I swing the wheel a full revolution back to the left, and everything stabilizes.

"What happened?" hollers John, as he climbs back up to the command bridge.

"Operational error," I reply. "I forgot I had the wheel turned nearly all the way to the right, rather than straight ahead."

I've lost the battle. John doesn't buy my explanation one bit. He'll never listen to my suggestions to dock this boat by using just the shift levers after this ruckus.

"Sure," says John. "Sure."

*****

THE REST OF OUR TREK OUT OF THE HARBOUR is without further incident. We both calm down, and I hand the helm controls over to John. When adequately clear of the breakwater, he pushes the throttles forward to come up onto plane. All is normal at first, and then the power on the port engine drops nearly to zero. John tries again, and again, but it's no use. The problem hasn't gone away, nor did either of us expect it to.

With both engines idling, we open the engine compartment, and John peers inside. He asks me to apply some power while he looks things over, but he finds nothing unusual.

"I think it's the fuel," he says, yelling up to the command bridge where I man the throttles.

He says this with a hint of challenge in his voice. Like he has an idea brewing, but it hasn't popped out yet.

"Let's find a place where there's not so many waves," he says. "Up against Harwood should work. Should be pretty calm there."

In the lee of Harwood Island, we anchor in 30 feet of water near the south shore. Once the anchor is secure, we shut off both engines, and John pulls out his tools. He tackles the small in-line filter on the port engine's carburetor, but finds no signs of blockage. While we bob in the water near Harwood, he checks the security of some other engine components, and rechecks the distributor cap. He's not satisfied with the job I've done cleaning the inside of the cap, so he uses a wire brush to clean the connections more thoroughly.

When he's finally done, we crank up the engines, and try again. And again. It's obvious we're beating a dead horse, since it's an elusive problem causing the engine to misfire only at high power settings. Bobbing up and down in the ocean isn't the best place to do anything more extensive, so we finally head home.

"I'll take it in," he says as we approach the harbour entrance. It's a matter-of-fact statement that tells me I'll never get to drive again.

John's first docking with the twin-engine boat is nearly flawless. I notice he uses all of the controls together, not asymmetrically as the experts prescribe. He operates the two shift levers and both throttles as one, and he uses the wheel to kick the ass around, just like in a single-engine boat. And, of course, it's a perfect docking. I just knew he could do this in his sleep.

* * * * *

THE ENGINE CUTTING OUT at high power settings proves to be an elusive mystery. John struggles with the problem for several weeks. He finds obvious deficiencies in the port engine, including a hard-to-get-at-it fuel pump that shows internal damage, probably from the passage of contaminants. His focus is clearly on the fuel system now, including the carburetor. He even suspects the fuel tank itself, although the two outlets for the twin engines should be producing a similar supply of fuel. One engine runs fine, the other still falls off at high RPM.

Finally, John swaps the hoses from the tank outlets, and the problem moves to the starboard engine. This is it! There's fuel blockage somewhere upstream of the outlet, which means either in the tank or the fitting at the tank.

The fitting is a check valve design. When you blow through it, the ball barely moves off its seat. So he replaces it with a new valve. This must be the source of the problem, and another acceleration test by John while I'm up the lake will prove the results. This is his sixth test run – undo the dock lines, disconnect shore power, maneuver out through the harbour entrance, test the engine, and then back to the marina. It's unsuccessful again, so he trudges back into the harbour, ties up the boat again, and connects the electricity.

"You must be getting pretty good at docking this boat by now," I relay over the telephone.

"It's about the only thing that's working," he replies disgustedly. "It's gotta be inside the tank."

"So let's go into the tank," I suggest. "I can meet you at the boat when you're ready."

"Oh, sure. Sounds easy. But not so. I tried cranking on the outlet nut, just to see if I could break it loose. That baby is jammed tight."

Too tight for John to loosen is plenty tight.

"I'll bring a torch," I reply. "Some direct heat ought to do it."

"Bright idea. It would take care of things, that's for sure."

"Well, maybe not such a good idea," I laugh. "But do you want to give it a try again tomorrow."

"Why not. I'll bring a big pipe wrench and a long extension handle."

"So what time do you want to meet?" I ask.

"About ten o'clock, but not if it's pissin' down rain."

Which it might be. An extension to the local summer has pushed warm, clear skies into mid-September. The conditions earlier this month would have been perfect for cruising on the chuck. I could have made it to the Broughtons, but the forecast for the next two weeks looks bleak. Abruptly, summer seems to have ended. My first season with the new boat has produced no ventures north of Cortes Island. Even if we fix the fuel problem tomorrow, the inlets to the north will have to wait another year.

* * * * *

When I'm at my cabin by myself, communicating with John is difficult. When Margy isn't with me, I often have only my American cell phone, which imposes extra charges for John (and the telephone has no connector to the cabin's rooftop antenna). To keep costs down, I encourage him to call Margy's Canadian cell phone, no matter where she might be. Margy then promptly relays the message to my voicemail. In the cabin, although I can seldom receive direct calls, I reliably get the message beep. After struggling for a few minutes at the corner of the float, where cell reception is barely adequate, I'm able to retrieve the message. If I need to reply, it'll be necessary to motor out to Chippewa Bay to make my calls – limited by weather on the lake or the onset of darkness.

Thus, when I wake up to steady rain, I decide to forego the telephone struggle. Instead, I simply head for town. Even if the rain cancels our planned boat repairs, I have plenty of city errands to keep me busy.

After arriving at the Shinglemill in the Campion, I drive to the North Harbour, phoning John from there at 9:45.

"Hello," says John, Canadian drawl.

"It's pissin down rain," I note without identifying myself.

"But not that bad," he replies. "The canopy on the Bayliner's back deck covers the engine compartment pretty well, so let's do it. Where are you?"

"In the parking lot at the North Harbour."

"Oh. Then I'm leaving now."

It's only a few minutes before Bro charges my truck door, leaping up to the window to get closer. He's on his blue collar leash, which is rare.

"I can't believe he's on a leash," I say to John.

"Rules, you know."

Oh, sure. John is big about rules.

At the boat, John positions himself in the aft cabin, where he can reach through the port engine's access panel. He maneuvers the big wrench into place, and adds the 3-foot extension bar.

From above him, spread out over the open engine compartment, I'm able to reach down and help pull on the bar while John pushes. Just when I think we'll never get the nut off, it rotates ever so slightly. The next attempt produces no further movement.

"We're gonna' get 'er," says John with a grunt.

And we do, although it requires considerable maneuvering with the wrench and bar to clear the protruding engine hoses and wires. Finally the nut turns freely, and John pulls it loose. The nut is attached to a half-metre plastic hose that can be lifted completely out of the tank. As soon as we see the end of the hose, the problem is obvious.

The tube's end incorporates a filter screen, completely blocked by a soft brown contaminant. This just has to be the source of our problem, and it's fixed in an instant!

We're confident about the certainty of our find, but there's still the test run. I disconnect the shore power while John warms up the engines from the command bridge. I remove the fenders and unhook the lines.

As I hop aboard, I thrust off with my foot, pushing the stern outward, and yell up to John: "I'm in!"

As John maneuvers out of our parking spot, I give Bro a few moments of attention on the aft deck, slip into the cabin, and then climb up to the command bridge, carrying two lifevests.

"You'd better put this on," I say as I plop down next to John. "Because if this doesn't work, we're gonna' sink 'er."

John laughs, but we're both in the same mindset. This has to work.

"Hey, I'm serious," I add. "We can climb aboard the dinghy and scuttle the Bayliner. Or just swim to shore. Think what we could do with the insurance money."

We head out into the open water. The sea is nearly calm, and the route straight ahead to the Hulks is wide open.

"Here we go," says John matter-of-factly.

The Bayliner eases up onto plane – smoothly, with no loss of power.

I'm yelling and screaming. John turns towards me, broadcasting a broad smile.

A summer of cruising has been lost. But there will be other summers. And the inlets to the north aren't going anywhere.

Chapter 11

The Tides of Washington

As a novice, I often wonder what boating is like in other regions. Coastal BC is a remarkable environment, but how unique is it? Is boating really that different in other parts of Canada, or even in other countries? With my limited boating experience, I'm certainly not the one to judge. But haven't you asked yourself the same question? – How different is nautical life in the Maritime Provinces, Florida, or even Australia? What would it be like if we could lift our boat from BC and drop it into the water near Deception Pass, a famous tidal narrows near Whidbey Island in the state of Washington?

* * * * *

I FLY MY PIPER ARROW SOLO from Powell River to Bellingham, where I join Margy for a week of book business and exploration of some of Washington's local airports. But the weather for flying doesn't cooperate. So instead, on a June day, we drive to Whidbey Island. Margy drops me off at the parking area just beyond the bridge at Deception Pass, while she continues to the Naval Air Station with her mom, where they'll spend a few hours shopping at the commissary and base exchange. I'll have at least 3 hours to explore the area below the bridge, where Washington's most-visited state park sprawls along beautiful beaches and the ocean is squeezed through a narrows roiling with tidal current.

Looking down from the bridge, the flooding tide spreads out below. The flow is pushing inward through the Strait of Juan de Fuca to the west. The current passes under the bridge and then winds south along the inside of Whidbey Island. Captain Vancouver passed through here in 1792, battling the swift flow and erroneously identifying Whidbey

View from Deception Pass Bridge looking west

Island as a long peninsula. Soon discovering his error, he named this narrows Deception Pass.

I hike down from the bridge to the small curve of shore called Little North Beach, covered with a natural pavement of small, smooth rocks. Huge driftwood logs rest confidently on shore, well above the high-tide mark. This could be a beach in coastal British Columbia, except for the numerous tourists dotting the shore.

People, in fact, are the first thing that strikes me as different. The beach isn't crowded, but families congregate along the shore, quietly enjoying the day. They huddle in small groups, never alone, for a few minutes of rest from a ride along the highway or on a short hike from their campsite in the state park. These could be Canadians, but they seem more like infrequent visitors who have come to see the ocean. This might be coastal BC, but it isn't.

The bridge overhead is also not British Columbia. The marvelous structure is busy with cars, RVs, and tractor-trailers – a combination

Deception Pass Bridge from Little North Beach

of tourists and business-as-usual. The traffic is continuous, providing a persistent background of human movement and the hum of road noise.

Current swirling off Little North Beach

The flooding tide is now well reduced from its maximum current of 5.5 knots, with two more hours before slack. The water swirls noisily, with a broken line of whitecaps within 10 metres (oops – yards) of shore. I sit on a log, listening and watching. Tides are a universal beauty. The power of this water is as obvious as the forces in Johnstone Strait.

How else is this place different from coastal BC? Besides the politics, this spot has a different feel. Yet this beach, even with its rounded rock pavement and background noise, is the same in more ways than it's different. A person who loves the ocean can easily see similarities – the direct influence of the tides and the current's constant ebb and flow.

Many who visit this beach today are inattentive of the sea's power. Unless you live at the water's edge or are on (or in) the water, the effect of the ocean is less evident. But those who live with the ocean, whether in Canada or elsewhere, feel the constant influence of its strength. Those directly connected to the economy of the sea, such as commercial fishermen, feel the power of the ocean even more – on both sides of the border.

The background sound of water flowing through Deception Pass, minus the nearby bridge traffic and human voices on the shore, could be described as a mild cascade. Military jets and helicopters occasionally zoom overhead, interrupting the murmur of the current. Two S-3 Vikings descend in formation towards Whidbey Naval Air Station, the scream of their turbofans distinctly different from the lower pitch of commercial jets. The babble of the water is momentarily lost in the background. This happens similarly (but less often) in Canada, and I admit I enjoy the interruptions caused by fighter jets from Comox in an otherwise tranquil coastal setting. But there are more jets here, with seldom a break in the action.

A brawny metal boat bursts out from under the bridge, headed out to sea. It's another reminder of the common threads of boating on both sides of the border. Until, that is, I hear the distorted blare of the captain's voice over a distant speaker. His words (or maybe a recorded announcement) are directed at the tourists aboard. I'm watching an eco-tour that seems out of place here. Still, it's a skookum boat.

I plan to witness the swing of the tides from this beach. That leaves plenty of time to hike to the other side of the narrows and back before the onset of high tide. So I start up the trail to the bridge. On the

Eco-tour boat

way up, I meet hikers headed down, more visitors who are never by themselves, moving predictably in small groups.

Halfway up the trail, a man and his son stop by the side of the groomed path to let me pass. I say "Hello," and the man smiles before he speaks.

"Boo, Trojans!"

Oh, it's my T-shirt, emblazoned with *USC*. This is University of Washington territory, bitter rivals of the University of Southern California. When I wear a similar shirt in British Columbia, no one seems to notice. Maybe its the American competitive style that makes today different.

"Go Huskies," I reply, in meek recognition of the home turf. But I don't really mean it.

Near the top of the trail, I look back down over Little North Beach, a magnificent view.

In the parking lot near the bridge, automobiles and RVs fill almost every available parking spot, precisely positioned between angled

Looking down on Little North Beach

white lines. A yellow booth at the edge of parking area boasts: *Jet Boat Rides – $15 per person.* That explains the skookum-looking tour boat.

I walk out onto the narrow pedestrian lane of the bridge, planning to take a photo from mid-span. But within only a few metres, my muscles shrink from fear. The drop-off below the bridge isn't my favourite thing, and this structure is particularly frightening. Acrophobia isn't uncommon among pilots, and I admit to a mild case. Looking down the side of a bridge, seeing the support structure below me, is different than the view from an airplane where I feel comfortably suspended in my metal cocoon.

I sneak back to the comfort of the parking lot, and then down under the approach end of the bridge. I hike the short trail leading underneath that leads to the other side, where I snap a photo of the underlying structure.

A sign on the trail reads: *To Summit.* I follow it along the high cliffs overlooking the other side of Deception Pass. This trail is wide and well maintained, but I meet no one as I head upward.

Underneath the bridge

Below me, through the trees, I watch a sailboat circling on this side of the pass, waiting for slack tide. The boat tows a dinghy, and it reminds me of similar scenes in the narrow passages of British Columbia where boats wait for the turn of the tide. It's an eager (yet simultaneously comforting) period of time in any boat.

In another kilometre, the trail splits. Both spurs are well groomed, but the path to the right is distinctly uphill and a bit narrower. The other trail leads downhill, so I elect to go uphill and to the right. This should be the route to the summit.

As I climb, I carry my camera in one hand and its case in the other. However, the trees are so thick, there's little to photograph in the shadows. Then the trail suddenly narrows, although still well maintained, and I question why I'm carrying my camera. Instead, my hands should be free for my knife, just in case. There are people nearby, but none are in sight, and the woods are thick. Wildlife undoubtedly resides within these trees, although probably not of the large, aggressive variety.

I remember John's story on the phone last night. Yesterday, he hiked a forest road on Goat Island with Bro. When he crested a hill, John heard Bro scurrying behind him. He turned to see what was alerting his dog. Instead of Bro, John stood face to face with a cougar, standing between him and the dog.

"He was big and scrawny looking. Hungry, I'd say," said John. "I did everything I could to scare him away – I yelled and swore and threw my arms around."

It worked. The cougar retreated to the side of the road, walking (not running) behind some shake blocks piled nearby. John followed for a brief distance, to make sure the cougar kept going. Luckily, Bro lived through an incident that might have marked his end if the cougar had turned the other way.

"I threw some rocks to keep him moving. My first toss missed completely, but the second throw hit him right in the ass. That got him going."

After the encounter, John hurried back down the road to find Bro, who was pacing wildly, sniffing the dirt. Apparently, the dog had picked up the scent of the cougar but never saw it. Lucky Bro. He might have become cougar dog food.

After this incident, John removed a knife from his backpack and carried it the rest of the afternoon. As John noted, it's a wise way to hike in cougar country. Pepper spray or bear bangers (explosive cartridges) are better yet.

These woods around me suddenly look like cougar country, and my hands are full of a useless camera and its case. So I stop, and put my camera away, extracting my puny Swiss Army knife from my backpack. It isn't much, but I feel more comfortable with it in my pocket, ready in case I need it.

I continue up the trail a short distance, but the path narrows substantially now. The summit is probably only a little ways ahead, but the climb is steep, and time is running out. I want to witness the moment of high tide, and the summit isn't important today. So I turn around and start back down the trail.

Overhead, I hear jets, high-pitched and definitely military. I look up but can't catch a glance of them through the trees. I imagine them to be F-18s, two in formation. And I'm probably right, since they have the screeching sound of military fighters, and F-18 Hornets are the primary fighter at the nearby naval air station.

I rejoin the main trail and pass the spot where the sailboat waited. It's gone, probably having decided to push through Deception Pass just before high tide. With the wind from the west, and the water flowing from the same direction, adequate control of the sailboat should be assured without waiting for the exact moment of slack tide.

I cross under the bridge and back down the trail to Little North Beach, hurrying now to beat the change of tide. When I'm finally able to get a clear view of the water below, I notice the flow has already reversed, although it's still five minutes before the predicted time. Tides are like that, even at well-reported locations like this. It's not an exact science, as the tide tables would lead you to believe.

On the beach, only a few people remain, but the pace of boating activity has increased substantially. The tour boat is speeding back under the bridge, and other vessels are entering and leaving the pass.

Water is flowing out from under the bridge, westward towards the Strait of Juan de Fuca. It's barely roiling, and the current seems somewhat confused, not sure which way to flow.

Eco-tour boat headed under the bridge

Boats converge at the bridge and push out from under it, a parade of vessels that have waited for this important moment. Two powerboats cruise past me, out to sea, maybe north to the Strait of Georgia. They look like any other Canadian cruisers, or American, or Australian.

Boats outbound after slack tide

The few visitors on the beach seem ambivalent, maybe simply uninterested, or not noticing the change of flow near slack tide. That used to be me, before I discovered the wonders of boating in British Columbia. I stand on this beach today watching the water, feeling the impact of this important moment in time. I'm meaningfully affected by the power of the tides, and I wouldn't have it any other way.

Chapter 12

Flower Rocks

"As soon as the weather breaks, we need to cruise down the Texada coast with the new Bayliner to look for flower rocks," says John one rainy spring day. "We can take the dinghy to shore, and just pick them up, as many as we want."

Flower rocks have been on John's mind for the past few weeks, but I'm not sure why. There's obviously more to the subject than I understand. Sometimes John is like that – there's the obvious reason, and then there's the reason behind the scenes. Give it some time, and I'm sure I'll find out what's really on his mind.

In the meantime, I spend a miserable few weeks recovering from the flu. It's one of those bouts that hits fast, and departs slowly. Although I'm technically recovered, my body doesn't feel right. I'm excessively tired – sluggish and unusually despondent. Since it's April, some of this may be my annual battle with the lack of sunlight that occurs each winter. Spring has been off to a struggling start.

During prior decades in California, the impact was significantly worse. Of course, that seems backwards, since California gets a lot of sunshine all year round. However, when the winter and early spring days are short, I'm prone to seasonal affected disorder, or so it seems. Since moving to British Columbia, the problem has been notably reduced. Backwards? Maybe. My theory involves being outside a lot more in Canada. So even though the sun angle is lower here and the cloudy days more numerous, I receive more muted sunlight in the winter. In any case, I've notice the overall improvement. But not this year.

So when John talks about chasing flower rocks, it has little appeal. "Where are these rocks located?" I ask.

"In some of the bays. I'm not exactly sure where. But they're really something. Smooth, shiny, and colourful."

So we'll be going up and down the Texada shore chasing rocks.

"A guy at the mill almost quit his job a few years ago," notes John. "He was going to give up his retirement to go into business collecting flower rocks and shipping them to Europe. They're a big deal there."

"You said 'almost.'"

"Well, at the last minute he decided to stay in the mill. Probably for the best."

"Probably."

"How will we know what bay has the rocks?" I ask.

"Oh, I'll find out in advance. Some of the guys will know."

Some of the guys. I just know there's more to this than meets the eye.

* * * * *

THE WEATHER REMAINS WINTER-LIKE. As April progresses, the storms keep moving down the BC coast and right over Powell River. There's occasional clearing, but never for long, and it's seldom warm enough to make cruising on the chuck enticing. The forecast flops around every day, not to be trusted.

"Friday is looking good for Texada," says John.

I'm consulting with him at his cabin, as I often do during a trip up the lake. We typically discuss a wide range of topics on days like this, but today he's focused on flower rocks.

"The forecast didn't look good to me," I reply. "The radio weather report says that Friday looks like another storm."

"That's changed again. Now it looks good."

This isn't like John. He never trusts the weather forecast (rightly so), and usually refuses to plan anything without the added skeptical comment: "Weather permitting, of course."

Today, however, he's ready to commit to boating on Friday. Something's different here.

"Well, okay," I agree. "But I'll be at my cabin until then, so I'll listen to the radio on Thursday night. If the forecast is for pissin' down rain, I won't bother getting up early and coming down the lake on

Friday morning. But if it looks like it might be good weather, I'll come down in the morning, and call you when I get to town. If it doesn't work out, I've got plenty of errands I need to do."

"Okay, but the weather should be good on Friday."

The new John trusts the always-fickle spring weather forecast.

With that settled (somewhat), we talk about the new cabin John and his friends are building near Squirrel Creek. Winter snow levels have been minimal, and work on the cabin has progressed nearly every weekend. After discussing this and a few other topics, I get ready to leave. But as I stand up and head for the door, John hits me with what seems like an afterthought.

"Jimmy and Francois wanted me to go riding with them Friday, but I'd rather go out in the boat with you."

"Oh." I'm not sure why he mentions this. "Where are they going?"

"To Texada on the ferry, but then they have to drive a long way to where they can offload their quads. I'd rather go out in the boat."

Quite a coincidence. Now I get it.

"So they're looking for flower rocks?" I accuse.

"Yuh, but we probably won't see them on Friday. I don't even know where they're going."

"And it's just a coincidence they'll be hunting for flower rocks the same day we are."

"Jimmy has some secret places to look for flower rocks – not sure where," John adds.

So that's it, and now it all becomes clear. It's a big race, and I've been drawn into these races before. Such events become pretty intense, and my body and its temporary spring rebellion don't feel up to the task.

In a similar race, John and Ernie were competitively trying to find a rumoured cabin, supposedly deserted in the woods near Olsen's Lake. John wanted us to get there first on our quads, and we did. But it was a grueling ride to win the race. John is very competitive, and he hates to lose. On the other hand, he almost always wins, but the toll can be demanding. Once John sets his sights on something, he refuses to turn back. I'm often only along for the ride, and sometimes part of the toll.

"So they're going to Texada no matter what the weather?" I ask.

"Probably, but we'll go only if the weather cooperates. There's no sense going out on a rainy day."

Which explains why John suddenly has so much faith in the weather forecast. He isn't going to lose the race.

* * * * *

On Thursday night, the radio weather forecast for the next day looks somewhat bleak. The operative word is "showery." Certainly, in my current sour mood, I wouldn't bother going out on the chuck based on what I hear tonight. Unless, of course, John is determined to go.

But it isn't a big deal for me to travel down the lake tomorrow, regardless of the weather. When I get there, I can call John and let him decide whether we should go out in the boat. The truth is, as grumpy as I am regarding the whole flower rock affair, I know it will be a fun trip with John. When it comes to traveling with him, by any mode of transportation, there's no other possibility – it's always a memorable adventure.

Thus, I arise early on Friday, make a final check on the marine weather radio, and head down the lake. Overhead, early morning cirrocumulus tell the likely story – mackerel sky, more wet than dry. It looks like it might rain today, but it's possible the sun will take command. The day could go either way.

* * * * *

"Hello. It's about time you got up," I announce on the phone.

"Where are you?"

I keep John guessing, with my constant movement up and down the lake, and to and from the States. He's usually surprised to find me wherever I am.

"I'm standing in the 3058, waiting for you."

"In the boat? Are you serious?"

"I told you I'd come down the lake this morning if it looked acceptable. But it looks like a crappy day to me, although I'm ready to go if you want to."

My negative attitude shows, so I might as well use it to my advantage in this race.

"Looks pretty good to me," replies John.

"Not really," I reply. "I bet it rains all day. Besides, it's gonna' be cold. Why bother with a trip on the chuck in weather like this? There'll be better days soon."

"It's not so bad. Should be sunny and pretty warm," says John.

"Looks cold and rainy to me. But I know you're in a race."

Sometimes it's simply fun to give John a hard time. It's hard to find flaws in his character, so I like to poke at him whenever I can.

"There's no race. We just need to go out and find some flower rocks. It'll be mostly sunny on the chuck."

It's not really a standoff. I know I'm destined to lose.

"Okay, okay, let's go," I finally say.

"How soon?"

"Right now. I'm on the boat, ready to start engines."

Once I get rolling when it comes to harassing John, I tend to overdo it.

"Well, I need to get some breakfast first, but I'll be there before ten."

"Okay. I'll be waiting for you. But it's gonna' rain."

* * * * *

I USE THE HALF-HOUR I HAVE BEFORE JOHN ARRIVES to set up the avionics on the command bridge. I mount the two GPS receivers, turn them on, and set the map pages. I zoom to a reasonable scale for a trip along the Texada shoreline. If I leave both GPS displays active until John starts the engines, maybe he'll use one of them. Normally, he ignores moving maps, since he doesn't trust them, and he knows enough about most of the places we go, so he doesn't need any other data. Even the submerged rocks in this region are engrained in his brain. But if the maps are sitting there in front of him, already keyed up, maybe he'll pay attention to them.

After I'm finished with the GPS setup, I relax on the command bridge until I see Bro. He's running down the dock finger, directly towards the Bayliner, charging hard to offer a hearty "Hello!" Behind him is John, his backpack slung over one shoulder.

"Looking more like rain now," I say to John as he steps aboard.

"It's gonna' be sunny," he states with a firmness that indicates this will go on all day, whether it rains or doesn't.

Bayliner 3058 at Westview's North Harbour, Powell River

By the time we're ready to cast off, it's mostly cloudy, but getting a little warmer, and still not raining. We take our normal positions – John on the command bridge, Bro on the aft deck, and me on the dock disconnecting the ropes and shore power. When the engines are both adequately warm, John gives me the signal.

"Anytime you're ready!" John yells down to me.

I unhook the last line from the stern, and push out as I hop aboard. Bro is pacing in the aft deck, crowding me as I step aboard.

"We're clear!" I holler up to John. "I pushed the ass out. Make 'er go."

John expertly maneuvers us away from the dock, backing towards the breakwater for a brief period, before shifting into forward and pulling into the narrow waterway, which is now near low tide. Rain or sun, mentally alert or worn out, it's still a momentary feeling of joy. We're headed out onto the chuck, free of the dock and making our own destiny. There's just something about pushing outward from a dock that always provides me with immediate elation.

Clearing the breakwater, we turn left towards Texada Island, and John edges the throttles forward until we're clearly on-plane. He raises the trim tabs to balance our load, and off we go.

We're headed north of where I expect us to go. Since I've assumed the bays we're seeking are on the east side of Texada (closest to our marina), I figure John will cut the corner and meet the shoreline near Van Anda, and then south along the island. But he's headed nearly directly for Blubber Bay, which indicates we'll be traveling along the less-traveled west shore of the island. There's nothing he's said that led me to believe we would travel the eastern shore, except he's repeatedly mentioned that it's a "short trip." In fact, just getting to the far shore will take a half-hour. From there, it's a long trek down the island, with no docks for sanctuary. I've traveled this side of the island only once, during a long voyage to the end of Texada, where Lasquaeti Island lies.

"How are we doing on fuel?" asks John. (The only gas gauge is downstairs.)

"Good. Only about an hour out of a full tank, so that leaves almost five hours."

"How far is that in klicks?" he asks.

Strange question. We certainly aren't going that far today. But John likes to confirm the details, and relies on me for the mental math.

"Let me compute it," I say, while mulling over the numbers in my mind. "Over a hundred miles on-plane, about 160 klicks" after making a rough computation.

"That's round trip, right?"

"Sure. Where the heck are we going?"

"Down the west side of Texada. I'm really not sure where to find flower rocks, but Jimmy says they're in a bay overlooking an island."

"You mean Lasqueti?!"

"That's it. Down on the other end of Texada."

"You've got that right," I reply. "It's the whole length of Texada!"

"So do you think we can make it on this gas?"

"Maybe not, at least not round-trip, and I'm not sure where we'd refuel other than at Pender Harbour. We'd have to go completely around the tip of Texada and then across to Pender."

"That would work," nods John.

Yes, it would work. But it's a mighty big trip, certainly a lot farther than I'd expected. Texada Island is an amazingly long island. I'm normally not particularly concerned with how much fuel we'll burn, since it's the cost you pay in order to enjoy the beauty of cruising on the chuck. Either you pay for the fuel or you don't go. With Canadian marine gas now at $1.30 a litre, it's best just to refuel when you need to, and not ponder the cost. But to burn a whole tank of gas in a boat this size to find a pretty rock seems vastly extravagant. I do the mental math, and conclude that finding a handful of stones will cost about a hundred dollars per rock!

"It looks like quite a storm down there," I say to John as we pass Blubber Bay, about to turn south towards our we're-in-a-race destination.

It does look dark around the point, showery in a brooding way.

"That's east of where we're going," replies John. "Look, the sun's coming out."

"Sort of, but I don't think it'll last."

On the other hand, this argument will continue all day.

As we approach the promontory beyond Blubber Bay, I notice John is closely checking the shoreline, comparing what he sees to the GPS map displayed in front of him. These are waters he doesn't routinely travel, and he knows headlands like this often extend underwater as lines of rocks, well out into deeper water. I watch him as he glances at the GPS.

"Does the letter 'R' mean rocks?" he asks.

"No. 'R' stands for reef. Rocks are shown by asterisks," I reply.

John nods, and comments: "According to this map, we could come in a little closer to that point, inside the reef. And I don't see any rocks on the map, right?"

I stand up from my seat beside him, and look over his shoulder at the GPS map. No rocks, and the reef sits considerably offshore.

"Looks good, if you want to cut it a little closer."

"So you think it's safe? You trust this stuff?" asks John.

"We can trust it. Let me zoom in a bit, so you can see more detail."

I push the zoom button, and the view is enlarged, still clear of rocks and shallow water.

"The shape lines up pretty good," remarks John. "You can see the next bay, too."

"Yup."

I'm afraid to show too much enthusiasm for this equipment, because I know he doesn't trust it. But to see him even looking at it for guidance is encouraging.

John cuts the corner, still remaining safely in thirty feet of water. After the turn, he points to the GPS.

"Another reef," he says. "But we can slip around it easily."

"Yup."

I'm smiling to myself now. As we continue down the coast, John watches the GPS more closely, bending his course to match the bottom contours. We cruise near the shoreline, providing a majestic view of the passing scenery, and John is enjoying comparing the moving map's features with the various indentations in the shoreline.

"Pretty nice to be able see things in this much detail," he says.

He's a convert!

The water is exceptionally smooth, with almost no ripples. It still isn't clear whether we'll run into rain, because the sky is threatening, but the going is smooth here.

We pass close enough to the shore that a large group of sea lions hear (or see) us coming, and slip into the water as a big brown mass. It's a fine day for cruising, and I have to admit it's comfortably warm on the breezy command bridge. For April, this isn't at all bad. Maybe today is the day my winter melancholy will finally go away. If so, I can credit it to a trip in the Bayliner.

Ahead of us, beyond the farthest headlands that we can see, sits a massive storm cloud. It's obviously raining a few kilometres ahead, and we'll have to pass right under this storm to get to the south end of the island.

"Reminds me of those TV pictures of tornadoes brewing in Mississippi," I comment. "Mighty dark, even a bit scary."

"It's still quite a ways ahead," replies John. Maybe even beyond the end of Texada."

"No way!" I criticize. "That storm is only a few klicks ahead, and we're just a little ways down the island, so far."

"We've come a long ways down the island," counters John. "Lasqueti must be just beyond that last point."

"If you ask me, that point is only about five klicks away," I argue. "We're not very far down Texada."

I have this theory – making this voyage sound lengthy (which it will be) and stopping short of the storm might cause us to turn around before we waste a lot of fuel and time. I know John is intent on winning the race, but maybe there's still hope we'll turn back.

"Must be close to half-way down Texada," replies John. "So we should be able to see Lasqueti pretty soon."

"I don't think so. Let's take a look."

I reach out to the GPS receiver in front of John, and push the zoom-out button twice. The boat marker is still too close to the shore to see any kind of overall scale.

"I'll zoom way out," I say, pushing the button a few more times.

On the electronic map, the north end of Texada now appears behind us, but the south end ahead of us is still not in view. So I push the zoom button one more time, and finally the far end of Texada appears. On the small-scale map, our little boat marker is barely displaced from Blubber Bay. We're maybe a fifth of the way down the island. I'm almost as surprised by our lack of progress as John is.

"We've come farther than that! Your GPS is worthless," he claims matter-of-factly.

"No, it's accurate," I argue. "Here, I'll zoom out with the other GPS."

I push the zoom button a few times, and the little boat markers on both displays agree with each other precisely. We're, at best, a quarter of the way down the shoreline.

"They're both crap," says John.

So much for his accumulated faith in GPS maps.

But the storm ahead of us hasn't gone away, and even John is expressing concern now. So maybe there's still hope we'll turn back.

If the mass of clouds is moving at all, it's headed directly towards us. Coupled with our own forward progress at 22 knots, we're about to get wet.

"Better stop for now, and let it blow over," says John.

I grit my teeth, and try not to smile. This storm may turn us back. And think of all the gas we'll save.

Once we're dead in the water, the wind stirs up almost immediately. Gusts kick the boat around, as we lie idle about a kilometre offshore. A few drops of rain begin, then hit with considerable force, big drops from towering cumulus clouds. Ahead of us, it's black. Behind us and to both sides, we can still see blue. We've left the side panels and Bimini top installed for this trip, but the rain is blasting in from the front of the command bridge.

"Let's go downstairs before we get wet," says John.

Down in the cabin, we wait and wait. Fortunately, we're now testing John's impatience. He hates to wait for anything, and the storm isn't moving through. Or if it is, the extent of the rain is nearly continuous to the south. In either case, we're idle in the water, with no end to the rain in sight.

"Okay, do you think we should turn around and go back?" asks John.

"Yes, I think so." I try to speak without enthusiasm, but inside I'm yelling: "Yes!"

The day is not to be wasted, as it never is when I'm with John. We've come out to cruise the chuck, and the weather back towards Blubber Bay is still good. In fact, after turning around and cruising a few klicks, we drive out of the rain into a mix of scattered cumulus and bright blue skies. Even the temperature is cooperating. Now that it's approaching noon, the thermometer has climbed to thirteen, a nice April day on the chuck.

"Let's try some beachcombing," says John. "We probably won't find any flower rocks here, but there's always lots of things on the shore."

This is more like it. No more racing. Jimmy and Francois have won. (Later, John smiles when he explains to me his friends didn't find any flower rocks either. They followed the mid-island road halfway down Texada, and then drove their quads to the trail dropping down to the shore where they expected to find flower rocks. But the path was impassible with overhanging alders and nearly flooded from the rain. They got soaked, and found no rocks.)

We pull into a beautiful bay near the old commercial kilns that have been shut down for decades. We drop anchor, and launch the dinghy, a task that takes a bit of time. First the inflatable boat is lowered into the water from its swim-grid mount, and then the outboard motor is installed on the dinghy's transom. Next we load paddles, and hook up the cruise-a-day gas can. Finally John, Bro, and I climb aboard and

Bro in bow of dinghy

cast off. John drives, Bro takes the lookout position in the bow, and I hang on for the ride.

Low tide makes it somewhat difficult to find a good spot to land, but finally we're all ashore. Then we climb over algae-covered boulders on our way to the rocky beach. The surface is both slippery and sharp, and I'm having a lot of trouble in my slipper-shoes. I notice John (who has no problems with his footing) doesn't say a thing. But there's no doubt he's noticed I've failed to wear my boots today, which makes the going tough. Bro, on the other hand, sympathizes with me, as he slips his way along the rocks.

Once on the beach, walking isn't much simpler. Less algae and smaller stones make the going a bit easier, but it's still an uncomfortable trek in my slipper-shoes. Bro plods along ahead of me beside John, who prances nimbly over the rocks.

As usual, John insists on a thorough inspection of everything reachable on the shoreline, looking for treasures. He hates to pass up anything he finds, accumulating long pieces of thick algae-covered rope, an old boom chain, and some heavy metal U-braces of undeterminable origin. To leave any of this behind on the beach would be against his ethics of beachcombing. If we've come this far, we'd better take it home. We look for flower rocks, too, but find none.

Meanwhile, my feet are hurting from the uneven surface. So I climb up on a huge boulder, and lie down on a flat spot that's big enough to accommodate my entire body. It may be a rock bed, but it's amazingly comfortable once my spine adjusts to the boulder's gentle contours. Meanwhile, John and Bro head in the other direction, going out of sight around the next point, still looking for treasures.

The sun is out now, so my resting place on the boulder is almost enough to put me to sleep. I look down at the nearby dinghy, where it rests in the low-tide waters. At anchorage in the distance sits the Bayliner, waiting for our return. It's always amazing how close to shore you feel when you anchor, and how far away the boat seems once you're on the beach.

Texada Island shore, looking west

I'm almost asleep when I hear John yelling to me, holding up some more tattered ropes and a faded life ring: "Found lots of stuff! Meet you at the dinghy."

* * * * *

ONCE WE'RE BACK IN THE BAYLINER, John explains (not surprisingly) that he'd like to make at least one more beachcombing stop. So we remove the outboard motor from the dinghy, along with our other equipment, and pull the small boat up onto its swim-grid mounts, roping it temporarily in preparation for the next stop. Once to shore today was fun. A second time may be more demanding than enjoyable.

We barely come up onto plane before John finds another bay that looks promising. We anchor, and launch the dinghy again. This time, I suggest that I stay in the Bayliner while John and Bro go to shore. John is reluctant – like the Marines, he adheres to the adage: "Leave no man behind" – but I convince him I'd like to just lounge on the aft deck in the sun.

"In the sun?" he laughs. "So you're finally going to admit it's sunny today."

"And really rainy only a few hours ago," I remind him.

Neither of us will admit defeat.

When John gets to shore, he yells to me almost immediately: "Hey, Wayne!" – holding a big black something-or-other high into the air.

"Nice!" I yell back. It's hard to feel anything but respect for a true beachcomber.

When John and Bro return, the dinghy is full of algae-covered stuff, including a black plastic barrel John thinks I'll be able to use at my cabin.

"You can use it for something, can't you?" he asks. "I thought you'd like it."

To get any use out of the barrel, I'll need to haul it to my truck from the dock at Westview Harbour, where the Bayliner sits on the most distant finger. Then I'll have to drive it to the Shinglemill, where I'll haul it down the dock to the Campion. Then the barrel will travel up the lake, where I'll offload it for use as… I'm not sure.

"Well, I don't know what I'll do with," I reply.

"Okay, then I'll keep it."

One thing for sure, he's not leaving it behind.

Along with a big pile of heavy rope, we stack these new treasures with those we found near the old kilns. The back deck of the boat is now pretty full, so it's a challenge to pull the dinghy up into position. Once again, we rope it off with temporary ties, since John isn't done with beachcombing yet.

"Let's try one more spot," says John. "I've always wanted to try that bay near the tip of Harwood."

"Okay, if you don't mind my staying aboard again while you explore," I reply.

"Sure, but you're missing a lot."

I may be missing a lot, but it's enjoyable just relaxing aboard the Bayliner. In fact, sometimes when I go cruising by myself, I'll often stay aboard the boat without going to shore for days on end, never feeling confined. It's part of what makes cruising on the chuck particularly enjoyable for me.

We cross over to Harwood Island, clearing "Becca" (Rebecca Rock) by less than a hundred metres. The sun is out in full force now, and quite a few recreational boats are on all sides of us. It's not nearly as busy as summer, but it reminds me that winter may finally be over.

We anchor in a picturesque bay that I too have wanted to visit. When I've passed this spot, it always looks so tranquil, and it never seems to be occupied by other boats.

The dinghy goes back in the water, we mount the motor again, and John and Bro launch for another beachcombing adventure. I watch them pull up onto shore near a big orange ball, a Scotchman broken free from it's prawn trap. There's no doubt this big ball is coming back to the Bayliner in the dinghy.

I kick back in a canvas chair on the aft deck. But I don't open a book. It's enjoyable just sitting here in the sun. I take off my jacket, lounging outside in a short-sleeve shirt for the first time this year. The sun angle is still low, but it feels penetrating, considering the date on the calendar. My winter blues are definitely on their way out, and I'm not about to stop them from leaving.

I watch John on shore, traveling back and forth to the dinghy, undoubtedly filling it with more things that are going to have to go somewhere. The rear deck is already nearly full.

When John finally returns to the Bayliner, he hands me a child's pink flip-flop sandal before he even climbs out of the dinghy.

"Look at this!" he announces. "You can put it on a key chain. It floats, you know."

I'm not sure whether he's serious, so I just say: "Thanks." But when he hands me the next item, I know I've been had.

"Here's a pistol I found," he says, passing me a small black plastic squirt gun. "Probably still works."

"A salt water pistol," I say. "Just what I needed."

The dinghy is full of rope and the big orange Scotchman, of course. The orange ball has black hand-written markings: "Tommy K," with a phone number.

"You can paint it up, and put it in the water at your cabin," says John.

But it really belongs to Tommy K. It's true that I provide sanctuary for a lot of floating stuff. My passion for floating treasures at my cabin is similar to John's obsession with beachcombing.

John hands me the mound of stuff he's accumulated in the dinghy, and I pile it onto the aft deck. I realize that there's no sense arguing about leaving anything behind.

Today's balked race, along with John's three trips to shore, has somehow brought me out of a season-long funk. No wonder Bro is always so happy.

Chapter 13

Boat Island

Over time, the Bayliner 2452 in Bellingham becomes one of my all-time favourite boats. Maybe it's because my stays in the States make me long for Powell River, and boating anywhere is a way to reclaim my British Columbia perspective. What better way to think Canadian than to go boating?

The 2452 seems bullet-proof. I've made more mistakes with this boat than any other (and you must admit, I make a lot of nautical mistakes), but this boat keeps on tickin'. There's no better example of those blunders than a long-planned voyage from Bellingham, through Deception Pass, and then back by way of Swinomish Channel to LaConner on a perfect boating day in May.

The morning begins busy as far as boats are concerned. At 8 o'clock, my friend Jeanne and I are on Interstate 5, on our way to look at a skookum 23-foot Jon boat with a 200-horsepower outboard. Doug, from Powell River, phoned me the night before, having seen a boat on Craigslist he's thinking of buying, and it's located near Bellingham. Am I willing to take a look at it for him, and stand ready to make a deposit if it's as good as it appears in the photos? Of course!

Doug is one of Powell River's mechanical geniuses, a guy who thrives on turning old boats into purring machines. This flat-bottomed, broad-bowed Jon boat seems perfect for his passion, and it certainly appeals to me. I can visualize Doug preening over this old scow until it shines, and tuning the engine to perfection.

Jeanne travels with me this morning because she's a novice boat freak – like me, except even less experienced. In her pocket is her Washington State boat operator's card, just obtained from the local Power Squadron: "Get your card, and maybe I'll let you drive the Bayliner," I kid. In reality, she already has considerable experience behind the wheel of the 2452, but she's still a newcomer, though certainly willing to learn. That makes her the perfect boating companion – enthused about boats, with a clear focus on boating safety. She'll never get me into trouble (famous last words).

But we've already been in trouble. In the first month after purchasing the new boat, we destroyed the captain's chair and went aground in Friday Harbor on the same day (Chapter 5). Of course, this is all the fault of the instructor, not the student, which is an appropriate way to view the situation. As a long-time flight instructor, I've experienced many student errors in the cockpit, but the outcome must always be borne by the instructor. After all, if a novice student pilot plows into a mountain with an instructor aboard, it would be ridiculous to blame the student, no matter whose hands are on the controls. Thus, it is with Jeanne and me – she may make the errors, but I'm responsible if things get out of hand. And on this beautiful spring day, that's exactly what happens.

* * * * *

WHEN I STEP ABOARD THE JON BOAT, I'm immediately sold. Even with the advertised problems (including a Merc that almost dies when you apply full power), this is a boat that Doug can turn into a valuable vessel. After the test drive, my biggest reluctance is showing too much enthusiasm. If I convince Doug to let me put a deposit on this boat for him, what will I do if he drives to the States to find my evaluation is totally wrong? Doug is the boat expert, not me.

"All I can say is the photos don't lie," I tell Doug as I stand aboard the Jon boat, talking to him on my cell phone. "I really think the engine is just a matter of cleaning the carburetor or changing the fuel filter."

"So you think I should buy it?" asks Doug, having more faith in me as a boat shopper than I have in myself.

"Man, I hate to say one way or the other. I really should just state the facts rather than my opinion. You'll have to decide."

Eventually, after I hand the phone back and forth to the current owner of the Jon boat, Doug tells me to leave a deposit. He'll come down to the States next weekend, do a compression check on the engine, and probably haul it back across the border.

I'm exhausted by the process, and it's only 10 o'clock. The excitement and pressure of this buying decision has taken its toll. Jeanne and I drive back down Interstate 5 towards Bellingham, headed for our already-delayed trip in the Bayliner. I've planned a detailed, time-specific voyage that will take all day, but once we're underway, it should be wonderful!

And it is. Sea conditions are nearly perfect, a warm May morning with one-foot waves. The route I've planned will take us through beautiful Deception Pass at slack tide, and then up Swinomish Channel, and finally back to Bellingham. To me, the tides in this area seem more difficult to understand than those of British Columbia. Low-slack at Deception Pass will be at 1:25 pm, while low tide at LaConner (in Swinomish Channel) is scheduled for 3:47. Since these locations are less than 50 kilometres apart, that mystifies me, and even seems "backwards" in terms of where the tide should reach slack first. Then again, the effects of winding through Swinomish Channel are noted for their peculiarity. The good news is I've thoroughly researched these tide changes (or so I think), and I'm prepared to sequence them for our route.

Our first stop is Anacortes, where we take on plenty of fuel to make it through the rest of the day without another stop for gas. At this point, we're slightly behind schedule, since I'd hoped to arrive at Deception Pass a full hour before slack. My original plan was to lounge on the aft deck outside of the pass, fishing and enjoying the picturesque location, but now we'll need to motor along promptly to make it to through at slack tide.

Sea conditions are ideal, so we make good time. Twenty minutes before scheduled slack, I slow to a stop, and shift into neutral in the shallow water near the tall bridge that crosses Deception Pass. I envision the faces of the many fishermen lining the shore looking out at the Bayliner, wishing they could drop their lines from our perfect location. But time is short, so after only a few minutes of jigging, we press on under the bridge and through the pass. Looking back, the immensity of this overhead structure impresses me.

Soon we're up on-plane again, headed towards the south entrance of Swinomish Channel. With Deception Pass now behind us, the time pressure is off. But I'm not familiar with this route, although I've been

Looking back (west) at Deception Pass

through here once before (in the opposite direction). So I ask Jeanne to take the helm while I consult the paper charts of the boating guide.

I'll be quick to admit I'm a GPS fanatic. Yes, I'm aware of the possible inaccuracies that can arise from reliance on electronic charts, but I've become accustomed to the power of GPS in cars, airplanes, and boats. Thus, as I consult the guidebook from the passenger seat, I keep an eye on the GPS that sits in front of Jeanne. Swinomish Channel sits a few kilometres ahead, where the channel markers extend out a long ways (and for good reason!). By my estimation, we're still a few kilometres from that critical location.

"Is this okay?" asks Jeanne, referring to our current heading.

"A little to the right would be good," I say, noticing the boat marker on the GPS map sliding out of the white towards shallower blue-tinted depths. White is good, and blue is normally okay, but it's time to pay close attention. Still, I know (or think I know) the channel entrance is still quite a ways in front of us.

Or is it. For a moment, I'm confused. The bow is pointed towards a jetty-like line of rocks that might be a mirage sitting on the now totally tranquil water. Or are those channel markers? If so, how can we be here so soon?

"More to the right," I say to Jeanne, still not overly concerned.

She turns to the right about twenty degrees. The GPS boat marker slides along the edge of the blue area, although aimed towards the safer white. For a few moments, all is well. And then, instantaneously, it isn't. It happens that fast – suddenly, we're aground!

Any boater who ever goes aground can't blame lack of warning on anything but operator error. That includes inside the breakwater at Friday Harbor the previous year, also with Jeanne – there's a trend here.

A terrible grating noise immediately tells me the boat has hit something, although it isn't yet clear what it is. Jeanne lets out a "Yikes!" and is thrust forward in her seat, her body covering the wheel and blocking my access to the throttle. My mind acts fast, as our minds do in such situations. We've obviously hit something and are still tearing through it. The boat is decelerating rapidly (as in "abruptly!"), but the throttle is still in cruise. Rather than holler at Jeanne to pull the power back and into neutral, I reach awkwardly between her and the seat, quickly finding the throttle and pulling it back. It's in neutral now, we're fully stopped, and the engine is still running. I reach for the ignition key, and shut it off.

"What the hell was that!" yells Jeanne.

"Not good," which is all I can say at the moment.

We both calm down, "floating" now in muddy looking water. We aren't moving, but maybe it's only the stern leg that's dug into the mud. I punch the throttle lever's tilt-trim switch to the "Up" position, and nothing happens – no trim motor noise at all. If the leg is jammed into the mud, it won't budge upward. Maybe the force of trying to tilt the leg has popped a circuit breaker. Maybe a lot worse.

When I glance behind the transom, there's a thrashed pile of mud peeking above the water about 10 metres back, where the propeller has driven through the sandbar. The only good news is I'm looking at mud rather than rock. But we're solidly aground.

When we hit, I didn't hear any ripping of the hull, as we quickly slid to a stop. And the engine was still running when I shut it down. Both are good signs, but the overall situation certainly looks bleak. I explain to Jeanne the immediate plan, but I'm not entirely confident it will work.

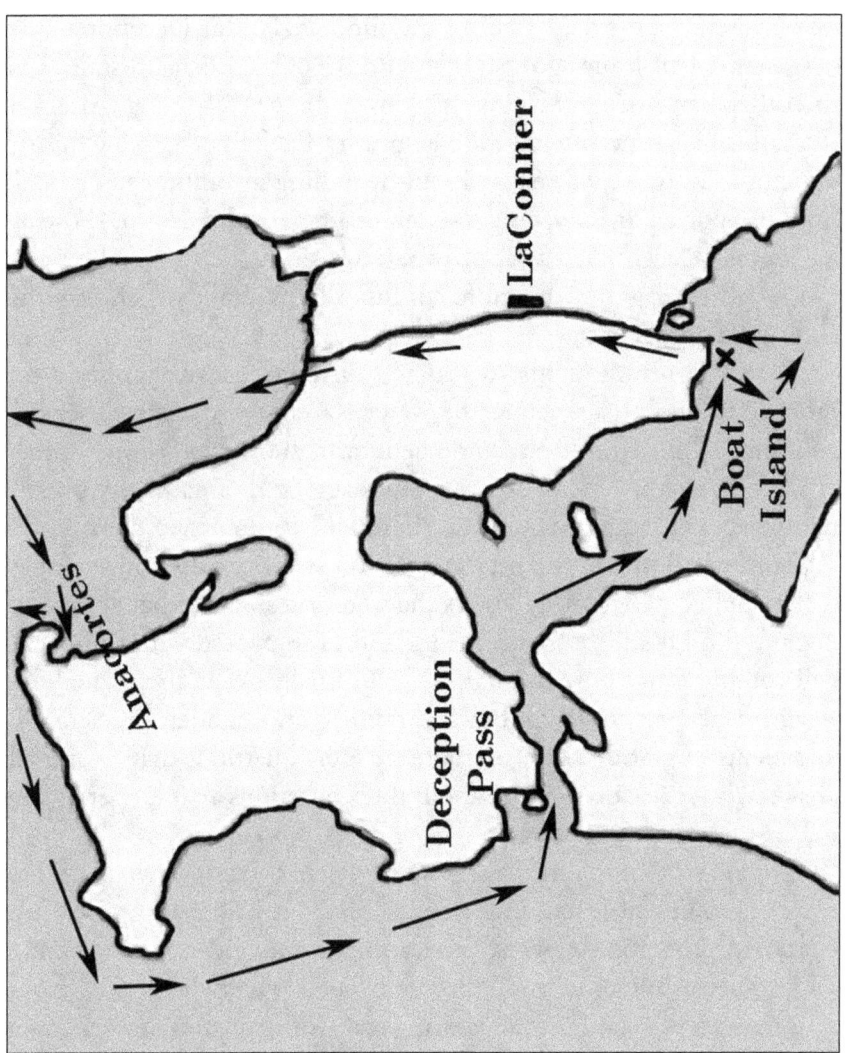

"The tide may be going up or down," I say. "Not sure which, but we'll be able to tell in a few minutes. We may be back in action very soon."

Yes, we do find out about the tide very quickly. But I don't like what I learn. The muddy mound behind the stern is growing in size, and now I can see a trench where the stern leg blasted through the mud. The tide is definitely going down. On the one hand, I know we're close to low tide, based on the time of slack at Deception Pass (less than a half-hour ago), so it should begin to rise again soon. On the other hand, it could be going down for several hours. After all, the published time for low tide at nearby LaConner is 3:47, nearly two hours away. I try to figure it out by pulling my author's notebook from my pocket and drawing a rough diagram of the region, showing LaConner, Deception Pass, and where we sit in the mud. The more I look at my diagram, the more confused I am about which way the ebbing tide flows here.

I explain my thoughts to Jeanne, warning her we may see a lot more mud around us before the water starts to rise again. Then, of course, we'll float right off, start the motor, and leave. I don't bother explaining to her that there are a few nagging doubts in my brain – like what will happen when the thoroughly entrenched stern leg is pulled upward by the rising boat. Is it stuck so tight that the transom will be pulled dangerously low as the water rises? And what about the engine – will it still run with the leg and prop packed with mud, and will cooling water flow through it? And, finally, what about the hull? – I didn't hear any ripping, but it certainly was a sudden deceleration and plenty of grating noise. So there are more questions than proposed answers, but I decide to think about these questions a bit longer before discussing them with Jeanne.

There are a couple of immediate concerns. First, now that we're firmly aground in a receding tide, the boat is beginning to lean to starboard. The good news is the leaning eventually stops increasing, and all feels solid. Second, there are boats everywhere today, but nothing except an aluminum landing craft (or strong inflatable) could safely reach us without self-inflicted damage. Even then, what could another vessel do except evacuate us from the Bayliner, and that would be a very difficult process in this muddy quagmire. Third, the numerous boats passing by might think we need help, and try to assist us, thus endangering themselves. As our boat steadies itself on the mud flats, we're certainly safe and secure for now, so we need to make sure no one comes too close.

I've turned off the electrical power to be sure we'll have plenty when it's time to restart the engine. An alternative to getting the main engine running is to use the kicker, which could propel us to safety once there's enough water to float again (and the stern leg is out of the mud). But the 15-horse outboard has been running poorly lately. In fact, one of today's tasks was to work on this engine, at least running some fuel additive through it in an attempt to clean the carburetor. But we haven't stopped long enough yet for me to complete that task. So the whole motor question (main engine plus kicker) gnaws away at me, while I try to concentrate on something more immediate – notifying the Coast Guard.

"I'm going to call the Coast Guard," I tell Jeanne. "We're safe here, but this is something we should report for a number of reasons. For example, one of these nearby boats might call the Coast Guard first, and that gets confusing. I'd rather explain our situation and our proposed solution, so they don't launch a vessel – at least for now."

When I say "at least for now," I notice Jeanne's eyebrows go up a notch. She has a lot of faith in my abilities and knowledge, which can best be described as irrational overconfidence. But I don't want to shake that confidence now, since her personal attitude is an important part of the success of my plan.

"Makes sense," says Jeanne. "We didn't really do anything wrong, did we?"

"No. Except going aground, of course."

She laughs, and that's a good sign.

"But who was driving?" she says with a grim look on her face.

"It wasn't your fault," I reply, and I mean it. "The only reason I asked you to drive was so I could obtain more information from the charts. I was clearly in charge, and the captain goes down with his ship."

"We're already down, as far as I can see," she laughs.

"Okay, I'm going to turn the electric power back on, and try to call the Coast Guard. The worst case scenario is low tide may be as late as 4 o'clock, by my calculations. Although, then we'll need to wait for it to come all the way back up."

"Good thing it's a nice warm, sunny day."

Good attitude. And I appreciate it.

My radio call is partly successful. I can't hear a clear answer from the Coast Guard, but I do catch a few words confirming they hear at least some of my message, so I try again, transmitting in-the-blind.

"Any Coast Guard station in the vicinity of Swinomish Channel south entrance, this is the 24-foot powerboat *Halcyon Days* transmitting in the blind on channel sixteen. We've gone aground in a muddy area near the south entrance to Swinomish Channel, but this isn't an emergency. We're undamaged and not in any danger, so we plan to wait until the tide comes back up, and then will attempt to restart our engine and proceed to LaConner. We'll contact you when this situation is terminated. No assistance is needed at this time, but please advise any boats that report our situation to avoid approaching close or they may become grounded in the mud flats. *Halcyon Days*, out."

This boat isn't really named *Halcyon Days*, of course, but the 2452 doesn't have an official name, and I feel more comfortable with a call sign. Right or wrong, I use that name on a variety of boats, although technically it's reserved for the Bayliner 2350 in Canada.

I wait for a reply. There's none, but I feel better to have transmitted. After another minute, I turn off the battery switch to make sure all power is conserved for our pending engine restart in a few hours.

Almost immediately, a small maroon metal boat slows down and comes to a stop about 30 metres behind our stern, which places it only about 10 metres away from our new personal (and still growing) beach. I step out onto the rear deck, and the boater yells something I can't understand. Our beach has small waves breaking against it, and combined with a little wind noise, we're out of range of even yelling conversation.

"Do you have a radio?" I holler as loud as I can.

No reply. I doubt he can understand me, so I go forward to the helm, pick up the VHF microphone and wave it back and forth in his direction. He must have excellent eyes, for I see him nod "Yes" in large up and down movements of his head. He steps forward in his boat, apparently to contact us by radio.

I flip the battery power switch to "Both," and send my message: "Maroon powerboat near the Swinomish south entrance, how do you read *Halcyon Days* on Channel 16?"

"Loud and clear. Do you need assistance?"

"We're fine. Our plan is to wait until the tide floats us, and then restart our engine. But we aren't sure our message to the Coast Guard was received, so we'd like to try again, and maybe you can hear their reply."

"Okay, go ahead," says the fellow in the maroon boat.

So I go through the complete transmit in-the-blind message to the Coast Guard again. Then I pause, waiting for the maroon boat. There's no response, at first, hopefully because he's receiving a reply from the Coast Guard that we can't hear. Then the boater transmits me a message that thrills me.

"Puget Sound Coast Guard says they understand your message, and they ask that you call when your situation is resolved."

"Thanks for your help," I say.

"No problem. Low tide should be at about 4 o'clock."

That too is good news. Although it's still over an hour away, at least it's something somewhat specific to look forward to, as much as "about 4 o'clock" can be.

"That's just what you predicted," says Jeanne. "You said it would be low tide by 4 o'clock."

"Just a guess," I reply. But I'm proud of myself for such a good (desperate) estimate.

We settle in, waiting for low tide. Our little perch, which we now call "Boat Island," is still getting bigger, and we're rising higher above the surrounding water. The many boats entering and leaving the channel pass right by us, and must know something is wrong, but no one stops. Of that, I'm pleased, but a bit mystified. Maybe it's more common to see a boat sitting here on its own small island than I imagine. Looking back past the transom, now with so much mud exposed, the trench carved by our prop is amazingly long and ominous. I visualize the stress that our hull and engine leg have gone through. If there are no leaks and the main engine restarts, it'll be a miracle.

The tide continues to drop, but I'm hoping "about 4 o'clock" is closer to 3:30. Both Jeanne and I find ourselves staring at reference objects near Boat Island's beach, trying to determine if they're getting closer to or farther from the water. I'm convinced the tidal flow has now stopped, and will soon reverse.

Stern track in the mud

We sit in the sun, and watch the constant parade of boats along the jetty that parallels the red and green markers leading into Swinomish Channel. I'm amazed how close we are to open water. So near, yet so far..

Nearby Swinomish Channel off the bow

"I've got an announcement," I say. "The tide's moving back in."

"Oh, I hope so," replies Jeanne. "The object I've been watching seems like it isn't changing, but I know we're near low tide."

This has been an amazing lesson for both of us regarding the power of tides. Never have either of us stared at the tide line almost constantly for two full hours, watching every incremental change. Imagine the immense power of tides applied planet-wide all day long, every day of the year.

The view from Boat Island

The reversal occurs later than expected -- approximately 4:45 – so that means we'll probably have to wait until at least 5:30 to get back to where we started. Then probably another half hour (or more) before we're floating safely again, unless the water moves up faster than it went down – which is the way it seems from our optimistic vantage point.

"It's amazing how fast the tide seems to be rising," I note. "It's like when you're on a long trip, and then finally start home. The return trip always seems to go so much quicker."

"I swear I can see the tide moving in as I watch it," replies Jeanne.

The waves on our beach are getting closer to us, and rivulets pour between the green and brown patches of mud in increasing velocity and volume. There's hope!

When the boat begins to float again, it's cause for celebration. At first, it's just a barely perceptible wobble of the hull, and suddenly the stern rises noticeably, almost level with the bow. I listen for unusual noises, like water running in through cracks in the hull. It's wonderfully quiet.

The boat is definitely floating now, and the water continues to rise fast. But were still locked to the bottom by the stern leg which is firmly planted in the mud. I use a pike pole to estimate the water depth at the stern – 3 feet now and rising, but I'm measuring from the swim grid, so the lowest "V" of the hull is probably still on the mud flats.

In the gentle wind, the boat rotates around the leg now, swinging smoothly, but we don't break free. Fortunately, my fears about the stern being pulled down as the boat rises seem to be an idle worry. But I'm growing impatient.

I send Jeanne into the cabin and all the way to the front berth, thinking the added weight might pull the leg up. Meanwhile, I use the catwalk to travel to the bow. This pushes the bow down, which must be putting more pressure on the stuck leg. With our weight full forward, the boat drops downward at the bow, but the leg doesn't break free.

I return to the aft deck, flip the battery switch to "Both," and then turn on the GPS (which also shows the voltage – 12.2, that's okay). The boat's position on the electronic map is right over a green wedge shaped area, and we're rotating on a corner of it. Once free, the wind should take us quickly towards the shore, but it's the wrong shore – the one with a shallow beach. I'll need to get the motor going before we drift very far. I'll try the main engine first, not wasting any time if it fails to start. I'm ready to immediately switch to the kicker.

The 15-horse outboard is hooked up to its cruise-a-day and ready to tilt down into running position, so I climb out on the swim grid and see if it's deep enough to drop the outboard. When I carefully tilt it down, the skeg hits the bottom before the motor is straight. So I pull it back up again.

Back at the helm, I watch the GPS intently. We're still pivoting on the corner of the green wedge. The GPS groundspeed flickers from 0.0 knots to 0.1, even 0.2, and then back to zero, probably indicating our rotation around the leg. It'll mean nothing until it clicks higher and keeps rising.

What seems like hours go by, but it's only a few minutes. Battery voltage has dropped to 12.1, and there's still no lateral movement on the GPS. When it's time to start the engine, I won't have time to monkey with the battery switch back behind me. So I leave everything as it is.

Jeanne and I are ecstatic. We're not out of the woods, by a long shot, but the water is rising, and it's even more obvious when I make another pike pole estimate – 4 feet at the swim ladder.

We break free, and I feel us drifting! The boat marker on the GPS leaves the wedge, headed slowly towards shore and another area of shallow water. Groundspeed readout is suddenly 0.5 knots. I flip on the blower, and without waiting the recommended minimum time prior to engine start, I hit the ignition switch. The engine starts on first crank!

I give the engine a few seconds to warm up before shifting into gear. This is no time to induce an engine stall. As soon as I hear the satisfying *clunk* of forward gear, I turn the wheel as far to the left as it will go. I want to exit immediately to the deepest nearby water, but I convince myself to refrain from adding any power yet.

The depth finder now shows 1.7 feet, then 2.0, then 1.8. It hovers this way for what seems like an eternity, and then jumps all the way to 2.9 feet. I push the throttle forward a bit, and then back to idle, visualizing the leg and prop traveling barely above the muddy bottom.

"Look at that!" I yell to Jeanne. "Three feet on the depth sounder!"

Usually I'm distressed by anything less than twenty feet, but not today. I'll take it!

We're both whooping and hollering now. I test the tilt-trim switch, and it still doesn't make any noise, but it's a minor detail. I ask Jeanne to take the helm while I sort things out.

"Point at those houses on the opposite shore. Just keep 'er going straight."

"You don't want to go back to our little island?" she kids.

"Not today!"

While I have a moment to think things through, I decide to secure the kicker so it can't flop around. I disconnect the cruise-a-day, and pull the fuel hose back into the Bayliner.

When I take the helm back from Jeanne, I try the tilt-trim switch one more time, and it works normally now. I'm ready to call the Coast Guard on Channel 16. This time I hear the reply clearly, maybe because of the extra voltage boost from the operating alternator. I report the change in my "situation," reminding them I promised to call back once we were floating again.

It's immediately obvious the Coast Guard doesn't have a clue what I'm talking about.

"*Halcyon Days*, go to Channel Twenty-Two Alpha."

I try that, but it doesn't work, so I return to channel 16.

"*Halcyon Days* unable Two-Two alpha," I report.

"Okay, let me know when you're ready to copy my phone number."

Not good, not bad – just not what I'd hoped for. I copy the phone number and sign off when they tell me to call as soon as possible.

"No sweat," I say to Jeanne. "Seriously, this is just like talking to air traffic control in an airplane – 'Niner-Six-Eight, give the control tower a call on the phone after landing.' In others words, they're moderately pissed about something, but not bad enough to chew us out over the radio."

I've been here before as a pilot, and this isn't going to spoil my euphoric mood. We're safe, the boat is in one piece, and the motor seems like it has dodged a mighty big bullet. I let Jeanne drive while I pull out my telephone.

What I haven't told Jeanne is my cell phone battery is nearly depleted. She's already explained that her phone thinks we're in international waters and shows no service. So I use my phone to dial the number, hoping the battery will hold out. A young-sounding male voice answers, and when I identify myself, it's a burst of questions.

Which Coast Guard station did I originally contact? Did I hear a confirmation that the station received my message? Exactly what did I tell them when I called?

I answer all of the questions as truthfully as possible, and tell the young man about my radio conversation with the fellow in the maroon boat and his confirmation that convinced me Puget Sound Coast Guard heard my transmission. Then there's another question.

"Do you have a depth sounder or a GPS?"

"Yes, on the depth sounder," I reply. "But it just flashes when I'm cruising at any speed above slow. And yes, I have a GPS. But let me set things straight. When you put a boat on the rocks, there's really not a lot of doubt about what happened, is there? So just put 'operator error' in that next box."

I say this without (I hope) any anger in my voice, because I feel good about everything, including my actions in a very unusual situation. If he wants me to admit I screwed up, there's no need to question it, but I did my best once the situation developed, and I'm okay with it.

He actually chuckles: "Okay, let me verify where I can contact you in case I need more information."

I give my phone number and add: "Now you're gonna' think I've got a big black cloud over my head, but my phone battery is almost dead, so I might not be able to answer if you call me back until later tonight when my phone is recharged."

He laughs again: "Okay, sir. I probably won't need to call you again. Now you have a good trip on up to LaConner."

And we do, to say the very least.

Chapter 14

Too Big to Fail

I mope around the cabin on a perfect July day, trying to make up my mind. So many times I've faced this same decision between two favourable outcomes. Leaving my cabin in weather like this, with perfect weather in the forecast for a full week, is never easy. But going out on the chuck is always thrilling, and thus the dilemma. The good news is the first step involves going to town, which I need to do anyway, so the decision can be delayed. I'll pack up as if I'm not coming back for a week, and if I'm back tomorrow, it'll be cause for celebration.

July came in like a lion, bad weather piled onto a spring that never warmed, and precipitation that couldn't seem to stop. I've never known summer to come so late, but now, on July 6th, the warm season has finally arrived in all its glory. Clear and almost hot, and an extended marine forecast of northwest winds, with only ridges and high pressure on the weather map. The day at the cabin is perfect, so I bask on the deck and accomplish some easy chores around the cabin. How can I leave these surroundings now, when summer has just begun?

Playing devil's advocate, I conjure up a list of reasons to stay home. Margy is in the States, and although I enjoy time alone on the chuck, it's a shame for her to miss out on a boating adventure. Besides the wonderful weather that entices me to stay at the cabin, the new boat still has some unknowns. The anchor locker, regardless of endless modifications, still won't hold all of the chain without jamming the windlass, so it's a two-person operation during anchor retrieval. I stand on the bow, while Margy or John uses the remote switch on the command bridge. My job is to yell "Stop!" and then slip down into the bow's open hatch to rearrange the chain in its locker. Even in shallow water, it takes at least three trips up and down to get the anchor properly stowed.

Thus, one of the two main items that sold me when shopping for a new boat (the remote windlass switch on the command bridge) is an item I've seldom operated myself, except during tests in the harbour. (The other gismo that sold me on this boat is the digital fuel flow indicator, which has stopped working at both helms, and even John can't chase the electrons down.)

Adding to my attempt to convince myself I should stay at home are the engine woes that were only recently solved. Should I really go a long way from Powell River with the threat of coming back home on one engine. In other words, I'm grasping for excuses. To add to the list, I contemplate how big this boat is, and how inexperienced I am with its twin engines. Docking is still a challenge, and this would be a solo trip without the assistance of Margy, my finest mate (shipboard and otherwise). I do okay at docks I'm familiar with, but this trip, if I travel far to the north, will involve new marinas.

So I've come up with a long list of excuses to stay home, none of which are worth so much mental anguish. It's simply another indicator of how much I love this place, my floating home on Powell Lake. Tearing myself away from here is always a painful process.

I water the floating garden, a thorough soaking in case I'm gone for a week. Then I soak the planter containers on the various decks, and climb the stairs to the upper garden to use the rain-barrel hose for the potato plants. I retract the gangplank, pull the tin boat up onto the dock, and secure the cabin. By early afternoon, I'm in town at an author's table at the local bookstore.

"Are you getting some time off?" asks Corinne, the bookstore manager.

She knows my lazy summer schedule, and I know how hard she works, so I feel a bit guilty, but never enough to consider giving up my semi-retirement.

"Sure, but I'm working hard here, for all of two hours."

"Must be nice," she says with a smile.

"How about you? Got anything planned for the weekend?"

I know her schedule, and she should be off for the next two days.

"Not really. I'll be working straight through until a week from Saturday, so I can go to Victoria and have some fun with my son."

"Oh," I reply, now feeling even guiltier.

I ask about her son and her plans in Victoria, and Corinne explains they'll be going to a rock concert together. She's the kind of friend I admire, and she helps me think young.

"What weather!" I add, as Corinne indicates she has to slip away to help a customer.

"I've already forgotten about last week and last month. Isn't it great?" comments Corinne.

It's true. When the rain goes on and on, as it often does here, it seems to never end. Then, when skies finally clear, it only takes a few hours to make it seem like sunny skies have been here for weeks. Gloomy weather is quickly forgotten, which is one of the things I love about this place.

After the book-signing, I go to the grocery store next door, and stock up on food for a trip on the chuck. My plans are now set, or as set as they ever are – I'm going to explore the Broughton Islands and maybe Knight Inlet, farther than I've ever gone before. Finally, I'll be able to do justice to a book almost complete – this one! I keep saying I'll explore the inlets to the north, and I keep returning to my old favourite spots around the Strait of Georgia. I need to document some distant adventures, which is a great excuse for spending hundreds of loonies on gas for a big boat with twin engines.

Back at my condo in town, I debate when to depart. I could leave today, and get an early start on the first narrow passage (probably Seymour or Surge Narrows), making it through the initial challenge of currents before anchoring on the other side tonight. Another scenario is to depart today, but anchor short of the first narrows, ready to go through tomorrow morning. I check the tides and currents, and the first option falls apart. Slack tide will be just before dark, and it would mean pressing on towards an immediate anchorage on the other side, which means rushing. I quickly nix the idea.

Even the second scenario (stopping short of the first narrows) falls on its face when I check the Internet. The "Big I" is my friend and my enemy. I love it – without the Internet my mode of writing and publishing would be impossible. And I hate – it seems to absorb most of my time and energy when I'm in town. So as the "Big I" slowly steals my time today, it becomes too late to depart.

The third (new) scenario is what I end up selecting. It involves a leisurely departure tomorrow, and then pushing through the first narrows at slack tide and anchoring on the other side for the evening.

But the next morning doesn't go as smoothly as expected. I'm still absorbed in finishing a publishing priority (the "Big I"), and I have a few more in-town chores. By 3 o'clock, I'm finally on my way to the North Harbour, lugging a small ice chest, a bag of food, and all the essentials for several days at sea.

I pull the front and side panels off the canvas enclosure on top, stow my gear in the cabin, and climb up to the command bridge, finally ready to go. While the engines warm up, I disconnect the shore power cable and the docking lines, and I'm off. My overall goal is to travel north to the Broughtons and Knight Inlet, but I seldom worry about the details until the bow is pointed in the right direction. I'll need to stop at Lund to top off the fuel tank, and only then must I decide on a specific route.

Sea conditions are ideal, with gentle northwest winds and only light chop on the water. The ride to Lund is fun, and now I'm sure I've made the right decision. Although it will be beautiful on the lake for the next few days, it will be just as gorgeous on the chuck. I'm finally content with my choice, and it's time to enjoy!

At Lund, I pump 179 litres of gas, and ask the attendant my standard survey question: "How's business?" Gas attendants around the world are the best indicators of nautical economic conditions, because they see the trends, and most have been around long enough to make valid comparisons. As recreational boating goes, so goes most of the rest of the economy. Conditions at docks and marinas haven't been good in recent years. Now four years into the global economic slowdown that began in 2008, my informal gas attendant survey indicates the world isn't recovering yet.

"Pretty good today," replies the attendant. "Yesterday, too, now that summer has finally arrived. What a spring, eh?"

"Not much going on before yesterday, I suppose."

"No, really slow. But now that the weather's turned, we'll be seeing lots of business."

It's an optimistic view, which I appreciate, but the marinas speak for themselves. Lund has recently installed additional floating cement docks that require a dinghy for shore access. It's a reasonable approach for recreational boaters, but I've noticed the cement extension is totally unoccupied today. Where is everybody?

Before I leave Lund, I take some time to reorganize things in the cabin, and remove some snacks and a bottle of flavoured water from the refrigerator, carrying them up to the command bridge, and then spend a few more minutes looking over my boating guidebooks. Normally, I'd ask approval to do this after refueling during the summer, when other boats are typically floating near Lund's fuel dock, waiting for space. It's rush-rush all the time during the warm months, but I don't bother asking permission today, because it's obvious – the gas dock holds only my Bayliner and one other small boat.

On the way out of the harbour, I munch on trail mix and potato salad, and enjoy my cold bottle of water. In the 27-degree sun, I drive slowly, savouring my mini-meal. I haven't had anything to eat since a breakfast of cereal and nothing else. In addition, I didn't sleep well in town last night, especially compared to how well I sleep in my floating cabin. So I revisit the whole concept of hurrying towards an anchorage for the night near Campbell River or Surge Narrows, ready to negotiate the first passage north at slack tide in the morning. As I snack on the trail mix, only a few kilometres from Lund, I give the whole concept of rushing some more thought.

I continue forward, barely above idle, eating, drinking, and contemplating. I love this region, the northern Strait of Georgia. Why am I planning to leave it behind? My thoughts deviate towards Rebecca Spit.

The spit and its huge anchorage at Quadra Island's Drew Harbour is one of my favourite overnight spots, and I manage to visit there at least once each summer, so why should this year be any different? It would be an easy place to drop a hook today, without worrying a lot about the finicky windlass. Heriot Bay and its fine restaurant are right around the corner, a short trip by dinghy. This sounds like more of the same. But it also sounds comforting.

As I idle slowly from Lund towards the island some call "Little Mittlenatch," because it looks similar to its bigger cousin to the west,

I completely revise my plans. I'll travel to Rebecca Spit for one night, maybe even two, and bounce around the area for the next few days. The pressure is suddenly off, and I feel great! One moment I'm headed to the big inlets of the north, mired in decisions about tidal flow and timed passages, and a few seconds later, I've relinquished these elaborate plans for a quick hop across the Strait of Georgia to one of my favourite spots.

I bring the big (to me) boat up onto plane, and mentally calculate a GPS course for Quadra Island and Drew Harbour. The trip is through wonderfully smooth water, an exhilarating hour of cruising in perfect conditions.

When I arrive at Rebecca Spit, the bay inside holds only a few boats. I drop anchor in 43 feet of water, using the remote switch on the command bridge. I watch the coloured marks on the chain go by, until my rode extends 80 feet. It's only a two-to-one scope, but this bay should be calm tonight, and I expect the holding conditions (in mud) to be good. It's the most flawless hook deployment I can remember, all at the flick of a switch!

I settle in, watching the on-going show on shore, as locals bask along the beach and frolic in the water in an effort to beat the 28-degree heat. An access road runs the length of the spit, and families picnic and swim in an atmosphere reminding me of the 1950's, at least judging by the style of most of their swimsuits. When summer finally arrives in Canada, it may be only for a few days at a time, but locals are quick to take advantage of it. It reminds me of a weekend many years ago in the water at Cottonwood Cove, Arizona, where Margy and I sat submerged for hours, trying to beat the 40-plus degree heat. It was so hot during the afternoon that we came out of the water only long enough to eat and set up our tent for the night. Here today, Canadians seem to be fighting heat stroke in a temperature far cooler than Arizona.

For the rest of the day, I read and do a little writing, and watch a DVD movie on my laptop computer. Right after sunset, I crawl into the V-berth and am quickly asleep.

I wake the next morning refreshed, after a better night's sleep than I can remember in a long time. I stay aboard the boat most of the day, cleaning up the cabin and catching up on a short list of projects

I've delayed for months. I've come up with a way to run my small gas-driven generator (which charges my float cabin's batteries during the winter) on the aft deck, running an AC cord to a pigtail at the shore power connector. Now I can operate the boat's built-in battery charger while simultaneously recharging all of my electrical devices, the most critical being my computer. I spend some time tracing out wiring that leads to the boat's AC receptacles, labeling them for future troubleshooting contingencies.

I spend some leisurely time finally getting to know a boat I've owned for a full year. This vessel may be bigger than my older Bayliner, but it seems to get smaller as I become comfortable with all its nooks and crannies. It's not too big, after all.

In the afternoon, I launch the dinghy, and swing around the Bayliner to take a photo of the boat at anchor. It's always interesting how different a boat appears from this vantage point in the middle of a bay rather than the normal position at a dock. I don't get to see her from here nearly enough.

Anchored in Drew Harbour near Rebecca Spit

Then I head to Heriot Bay for lunch. I've used the inflatable with its 5-horsepower outboard only a few times, and seldom on-plane. Under almost perfect conditions in the bay, I bring the Merc to full throttle, but the dinghy just mushes along, plowing water because of my weight in the rear. I can slide forward only so far without losing my grip on the tiller, so I move as far as I can, and stretch a little farther. It's enough to barely get me up onto plane, but once I'm there I move back a bit and remain on the step.

The boat moves along well now, but no sooner do I get set in cruise than a small stick appears directly off the bow. It seems no big deal, since boats usually push small sticks away. Besides, I don't have time to turn, since I'm just now positioning myself on the inflatable's side tube. But the stick goes directly under the inflatable and strikes the prop. *Bam!* – the engine surges, and the dinghy swings wildly to the right, since that's were my weight is concentrated. Water starts to pour in over the rear gunnel on my side of the boat. I reduce the throttle to idle, and all settles down. I've been up on-plane only 10 seconds before I almost sink the dinghy.

I glance down at the red lanyard connecting the motor's cutoff switch to my yellow life vest. I wonder if it would have shut the engine off if I'd gone overboard. I've failed to test it, so I make a mental note to do so as soon as I get to the dock.

I take the dinghy back up to cruise by opening the throttle and moving forward again. Once stable again, I slide back along the inflatable's side tube, and cruise to Heriot Bay without further mishap.

At the fuel dock, I find a spot that looks out of the way, remembering to test the shutoff switch by giving a pull on the lanyard. The engine shuts off as it should. I tie up near the fuel dock, but there's no attendant to verify this is an acceptable place to park. Not only is this an expectedly busy day in July, it's a sunny weekend, when you'd think the level of activity would be extreme. I'm beginning to doubt this four-year mini-depression in the nautical economy will ever end. Even if it does, it's hard to imagine things returning to normal again. Then again, it makes traveling in the midst of summer a lot less congested.

At the restaurant on the hill, I eat on the deck, one of my favourite spots. As usual, the food is excellent, enhanced by the inn's historic

Dinghy at Heriot Bay's fuel dock (ferry pilings to right)

character and the beauty of the marina below. Familiarity breeds contentment, of course, although it also prevents me from traveling farther north.

After lunch, I visit the gift shop, where the bookshelves are empty of *Up the Strait*. I consider asking the proprietor if she'd like more copies, since it's been several years since I placed my books here. But she's probably a new owner, and won't remember my book. Besides, I'd have to go back to the Bayliner for copies. These are among the normal excuses I use to avoid interaction with business owners. If Margy was with me today, I'm sure she'd take it on herself, as she normally does. I may be a prolific writer, but I'm definitely a wimpy salesman.

The rest of the afternoon at anchor is a relaxing repeat of the day before – more families on the beach, boats coming and going in the bay, while I enjoy relaxing, reading, and writing. The evening cools off again, like it did the night before, making sleeping a simple behavior rather than the demanding endeavor it seems to be at the condo in Powell River.

* * * * *

THE NEXT MORNING, I amaze myself. I decide to stay in the same spot for another day. Two days ago, I thought I was headed north to Knight Inlet. Today I'm content to stay in place only a 100 kilometres from home. I'm really enjoying myself, similar to the relaxed feeling I have at my float cabin. I simply don't want to leave.

By now I've really settled into my comfort zone. The boat's cabin is getting cluttered, since I've brought stuff out of hiding and put it to use. Of course, I'll need to pack it all away again when I finish this "cruise," but for now it makes me feel comfortable to have some tools handy for routine maintenance and cleanup projects that I'm tackling. The satellite radio from the cabin is now set up and operational, dishes and silverware have been pulled out, and recharging cords for my electronic gismos are everywhere, powered by the small generator when needed. The dinghy now rides behind the Bayliner, tied and swinging with its outboard motor and cruise-a-day fuel tank ready to go at a moment's notice.

I work at cleanup projects and write a few chapters on my laptop. Mid-afternoon, I look over the boating magazine articles I've previously saved and placed in the front page of my 3-ring cruising

At anchor in Drew Harbour

guide, searching for a write-up I remember about a restaurant or cafe near the Taku Resort, directly across from where I'm anchored in Drew Harbour. Although I can't find what I'm looking for, I clearly remember an announcement about a new restaurant that was rated very high in terms of food quality and price. Maybe it was a bakery, like Nancy's in Lund. I also remember a statement indicating the cafe atmosphere was even better than the self-serve nook at the Taku Resort Inn. When I get to shore, I'll be able to find this new place, I'm sure. Then again, if the article was more than a year old, who knows if the place is still in business?

As I'm planning my little excursion across the bay, I also remember how good the food and atmosphere is at Heriot Bay. But I need to do something different today. Being at anchor for two days in the same place is fine, but I shouldn't repeat everything today, including where I eat lunch.

I hop aboard the dinghy for the short trip to Taku Resort. With the inflatable and its outboard motor already floating behind the Bayliner, it's like jumping into my boat at the cabin for a trip to town – everything is standing by and ready for action, an enjoyable situation at any anchorage.

When I arrive at the resort's marina, I'm not about the entrance, since there seem to be two entries. The one I'm closest to (the south end) doesn't appear to be an open route, so I proceed to the north entrance. This requires me to pass parallel to big old yacht, over 100 feet long, with "1943" on the smokestack. I imagine there are crew or passengers aboard who are saying the same thing I say when visitors cruise close to my floating cabin: "Damn Lookie-Loo's!"

When I get to the other entrance, it seems like the wrong way in. Maybe this is where the rental kayaks depart, but it might not be deep enough for the Bayliner. So I turn around and pass (again) parallel to the big yacht in the opposite direction, up close and personal. (Lookie-Loo's!)

I weave my way into the small marina, not worried about where to park, since the place seems rather empty. I tuck in behind a twin-engine inflatable with RCMP markings, which causes me to make a mental note to make a copy of my boat operator's card for future trips in the dinghy.

I hop onto the dock (literally), and begin to tie up my lines. The wharf is old but solid, made of wood, and I'm not sure if it's floating. If it's attached to pilings, I may be surprised when I return to my little boat. That happened to me once at Savary Island, and I had to go for a swim to retrieve *Mr. Bathtub's* line from a piling (*Up the Strait*, Chapter 2). In that case the tide rose while I was on shore. Today, it seems just the opposite – the tide is near the high mark, and is going down. So if I tie to the dock and it's not floating, I'd better leave lots of slack, which I do.

After I'm done with my line connections, I stand up and walk past the RCMP inflatable, which is tied with no slack at all, obviously indicating this dock is floating. I leave my lines slack, since there's nothing to hit but the RCMP – bow-to-bow inflatable tubes (and imagine the great insurance they must have). I laugh to myself about the thought. Fortunately, it's not a problem; I have plenty of clearance from the RCMP's boat.

As I climb the gangway to shore, the combined kayak rental agent and dock attendant asks if I need any help.

"No," I reply. "I'm fine, if it's okay to leave my dinghy here for an hour or two."

"No problem. You're good."

I ask my normal survey question, but I don't get a countable answer. "How's business?"

"Pretty good, I guess. It's my first year here."

"Well you sure picked a pretty place."

"That's for sure," he replies. "Last week three orcas come into the harbour, pretty rare here, as I understand it."

"Not very deep is it?" (Later, on the way out of the anchorage, I check my depth sounder; my maximum sounding is 98 feet.)

"No, pretty shallow. Two days after the orcas, a humpback came in. Would you believe it?"

"Must have been quite a site."

"Everything stopped around here. Of course, it never goes too fast anyway."

Which provides me with the perfect opportunity to ask a guy who obviously knows.

"Do you know where I can find a good place to eat, within walking distance?"

"Sure. Up the hill to the first intersection. Turn right to the inn."

I remember from the article – at least I think I remember – the Taku Resort Inn has only a self-serve counter, but even that would be okay. The dock attendant didn't mention the new bakery, and I don't ask. Maybe my free parking is contingent upon sharing wealth with his employer. There should be signs up the hill, or maybe I can see the bakery from there, or maybe there will be someone else to ask.

The big gangway splits around a large building that looks like the lodge, although there are no signs. I continue up the hill on a paved road, slowing to examine a few trails jutting off to both sides. They look like dead ends, and not big enough for a car. So surely the dock attendant means the intersection farther up the road.

It's a bit of a climb, and it's hot. I take off my hat and sunglasses to let myself sweat in the open air, and resolve to increase my exercising loops around the float cabin deck when I get home. I need the exercise today, but not the sweat.

At the top of the hill, there's an obvious intersection, with only one sign: *Thanks for Visiting Taku Resort*. So I'm leaving the resort, but still haven't found the inn, which seems like a funny arrangement. There's no sign of a bakery in any direction, so I start down the road to the right, where I encounter another sign: *To Ferry*.

At first, this confuses me, since there's only one ferry on this side of the island, which seems to mean one of two things: either this is signage to follow all the way across the island to the east side, where the Campbell River ferry connects; or this is the road to Heriot Bay. That's interesting, but not particularly of concern. The next sign is what I'm looking for – on my left is a big structure with a sign protruding out from the forest: *Food*.

When I walk close enough to see the building beyond the trees, I'm shocked. The "food" is a grocery store, and it looks awfully familiar. In fact, why would there be two grocery stores on the same end of this sparsely populated island? I've been to the store just above Heriot Bay, and this is it!

So after motoring across Drew Harbour to Taku Resort, I've hiked all the way over to Heriot Bay. The inn the dock attendant referred to was the Heriot Bay Inn, where I ate yesterday. I'd asked for a good place to eat, and he sent me directly there. Which is a lot like being back where you started.

*****

THE NEXT MORNING, according to the marine radio, a quasi-stationary ridge remains parked over the offshore waters, and the forecast is for more clear and warm weather. I come up with a new plan. While glancing through my cruising guide the previous day, I read about Quathiaski Cove on the other side of Quadra Island, opposite Campbell River. It would be a short trip, and the public wharf at the Quathiaski ferry terminal looks interesting, with a pub nearby. Of course, my favourite cruising guide is now 10 years old. Most of the anchorages haven't changed, but it's hard to know what to expect regarding docks, marinas, and restaurants.

I secure the boat for cruising, which means removing the outboard motor and stowing it, pulling the dinghy up onto the swim grid, recovering the satellite radio antenna from the bow, and a lot of reconfiguring in the cabin so things won't go flying around. I'll retrieve the anchor from the bow using the foot switch, so I can be ready if (when) the chain jams, and then I can slide it into its locker just forward of the V-berth.

As I get ready to hoist anchor, I reflect on the size of this boat. Standing on the bow, it feels comfortable rather than overly large. A boat I've always thought might be too big is finally just right.

It takes three trips down through the forward hatch to spread the chain out. By then I've retrieved enough to pull the anchor off the bottom, and I'm able to back away from shore. Once I'm in deeper water, I sort out the pile of chain. I winch in the rest, and redistribute it in the locker. John and I will need to put our heads together to figure out a new interior design for this stowage compartment.

Rounding the point at the end of the spit, I push both throttles forward, and the Bayliner goes up onto the step. I aim along the shoreline, watching the GPS for shallow water, but the biggest danger here involves commercial fishing boats near shore. Today two of them appear to be dragging nets, and there's an assortment of floating markers outlining their territory. After navigating outside this area, I

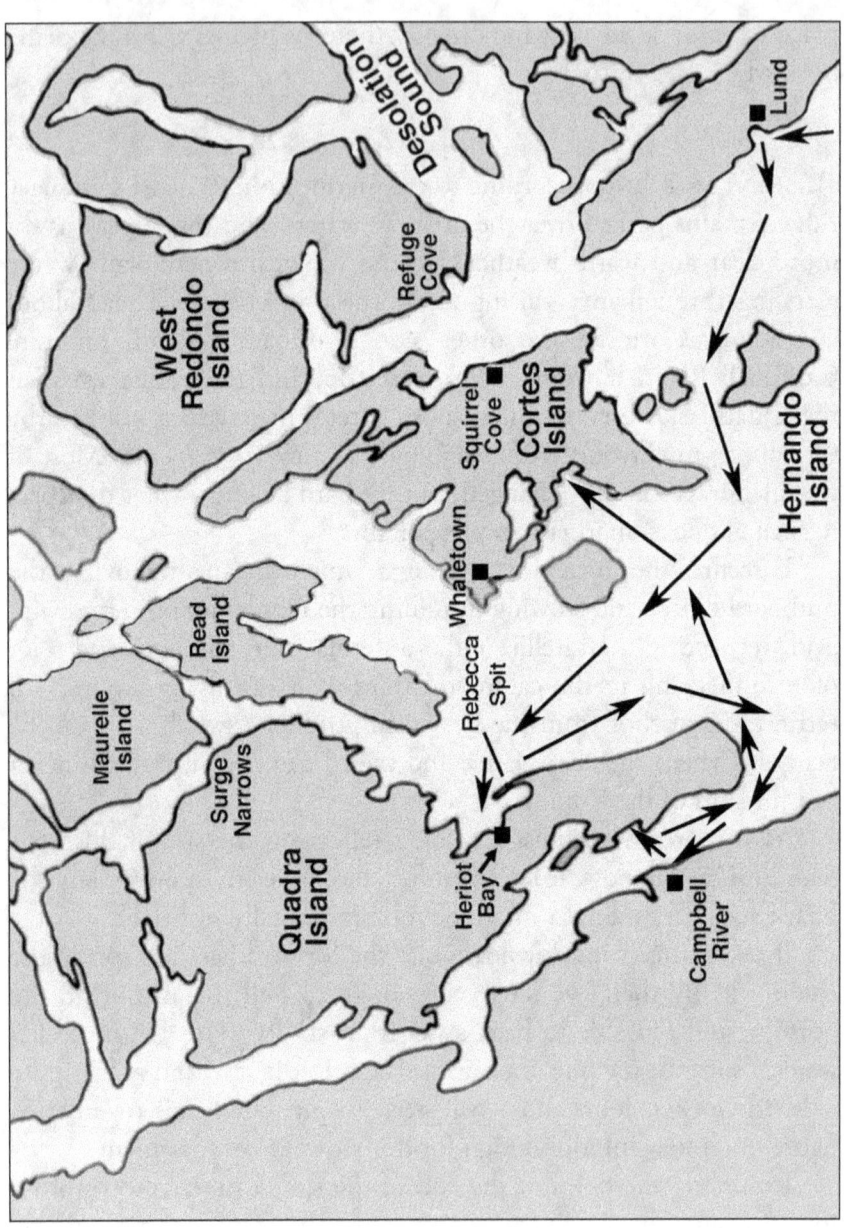

slide in closer to shore, until widening outward again for the shallow water that extends south from Cape Mudge.

Discovery Passage is always an interesting place, especially when you haven't been near dense boat traffic for a while. Today, even though it's near high tide, the current swirls as it always does in this area. The Bayliner feels the flow as we cross 6-inch standing waves with whitecaps. When you see small waves breaking like this, you know you're in an area of major currents.

I don't need fuel, but it's always nice to go home with nearly full tanks, ready for the next trip. So I gas up at Campbell River's Discovery Harbour, where there's quite a bit of traffic at the fuel dock. A recreational trawler is just pulling in to the smaller dock, so I go for the big wharf, where I have to step up to the fueling area bounded by huge tires used as fenders. I impress myself with a perfect port-side docking, but it helps that this is a familiar place.

After topping off the tanks, the trip across Discovery Passage to Quathiaski Cove takes only a few minutes, and there are several open spots at the government dock. I decide to go in close to shore, which should minimize the wake from the ferry when it arrives and departs.

I slide into a parallel parking spot under perfect conditions – not a breath of wind – and a young fellow comes over to assist. I throw him a stern line, and I'm quickly secured right where I want to be against the dock.

Arrival at Quathiaski Cove

Docked at Quathiaski Cove

"Do you think it's okay to park here for a while?" I ask.

"Sure. I'm the wharfinger, and you can stay as long as you like."

"Great. I wasn't sure there would be any space, but I wanted to try this place anyway. Can I stay overnight?"

"No problem," he replies. "It comes and goes around here. Depends on whether the fishing fleet is in or out. I hope you weren't expecting shore power, because there ain't none."

"I'm good just like this."

The wharfinger quotes a price per-foot for overnight parking, and says to come up to his office to pay, after I get settled.

"It's 32 feet, including the dinghy extension," I tell him.

"It'll work out to something less than 20 dollars, cash only," he says.

I really hadn't been paying attention to the per-foot price, since I plan to stay anyway, but I know I have some cash in my pocket. So I reach in, feel two bills, and pull them out. I hand him a twenty.

"Stop by and I'll have a receipt for you, along with your change."

"Thanks for your help."

He nods and walks away, but a few minutes later, he's back with the change and a receipt for $18.24, including HST.

"If you think it'd be okay, I might stay two nights."

"Sure. Just let me know tomorrow. The grocery store is right up the road, and the pub's over there." He points past the line of cars easing their way onto the ferry.

This place feels right, and I'm pretty sure I'll stay another day.

* * * * *

APPROACHING MIDNIGHT, I watch the end of a movie on my laptop. The ferry is in for the night, and the sea conditions in the cove are calm. Suddenly, a huge wave lifts the Bayliner so high that I'm looking down at the big seiner fishing boat moored across the dock. I grab the built-in shelf next to me and hold on tight. Then, after rising several metres, I'm on the way down, and the seiner is on the way up. The big boat seems to come almost completely above the dock, before dropping back down as I start up again in a powerful dance.

"Whoa!" I yell to myself, and after a few seconds all settles down, with smaller and smaller swells each time.

I look behind me. Maybe a big cruise ship is passing by, but he's already gone. The ship's big wake would have taken several minutes to get here, and long enough for the boat to cruise out of sight of the narrow cove. Or could it be a tidal bore, like the one I experience in Bute Inlet just above Arran Rapids (*Up the Lake*, Chapter 14)? Campbell River certainly has strong tidal flow, especially with Seymour Narrows just to the north.

I check my tide tables. Sure enough, it's almost exactly high tide, and it's a particularly high one tonight. So it must be a tidal bore. Or so I conclude until I see the wharfinger the next morning.

"Let me tell you about a weird rogue wave last night," I say, as the wharfinger nestles his clipboard in his armpit.

"Cruise ship," he says, before I can explain any further.

"Oh. I thought so at first, but then I checked my tide tables, and it was almost exactly high tide."

"Cruise ship," he says again. "They go by here in the middle of the night, and it's only a klick to the center of the channel. Let's see...

at high tide, he'd be passing south through Seymour Narrows after catching the end of high tide, and then grabbing the beginning of the ebb near Mitlenatch, where the direction changes coming around Vancouver Island."

"Makes sense to me," I reply.

I know about the big currents in Seymour Narrows and the change of flow around Vancouver Island near Mitlenatch. So I'm right, and I'm wrong. It was the timing of the tides that destined the passage of the cruise ship.

"Oh, I'm gonna' be pressing on today," I add. "Nice place – the kind my wife would love – so we'll be back."

He gives me a solid thumbs up with both hands, pulls his clipboard out from under his armpit, and continues down the dock, checking parking slips.

* * * * *

So I decide to move on. This dock isn't the same as being anchored, of course. For some, swinging on the hook is the best way to go, and I'm a bit uncomfortable here. Not disturbingly confining, just not as relaxed as when anchored. The convenience of restaurants and a grocery store is nice (along with a great Q-Beans coffee shop at the entrance to the marina where the ferry terminal sits), but that means people. I can sit here and write on my laptop, with all the windows and hatches wide open, but people pass by. Swinging on the hook for three days leaves me spoiled.

As I'm eating a bowl of cereal in the Bayliner's cabin, a young boy and girl, with their mother and a little dog on a leash, walk past the boat. But not in that order, for the little girl is lagging behind checking all the boats closely. I stand at the Bayliner's windows closest to the dock, and wait for her to walk past. Not unexpectedly, she peers into the Bayliner, and I stare back through the open window, only a metre away. The little girl is carrying a paper cup, and it's obvious she's intent on examining all of details around her.

"Is that coffee?" I ask.

"No." She shows me a pouty face. "I'm not old enough."

"You must be about sixteen."

"Sixteen!? No, I'm seven."

"Oh, seven. Do you like boats?"

"Yes. I went camping in one once with my dad."

By now mom, the dog, and the little boy are almost out of sight, farther out on the dock.

"Do you want to ask your mom if you can come aboard?"

She says nothing, but runs down the dock to convince her mother it's okay to come aboard. The three of them (plus dog) walk back to the Bayliner, and I invite them aboard. Mom and dog are content on the dock.

The two kids explore the cabin, and we talk about boats. They love the inflatable dinghy. We climb up to the command bridge, and the little boy gets to sit in the captain's chair.

"Do you live here?" asks the little girl.

"No, I live in Powell River. Do you know where that is?"

She shakes her head: "No."

"Well, I bet you've been to Campbell River, and Powell River is a little farther than that." I gesture to the south. "Have you been to Campbell River?"

"No."

At this I'm perplexed. She's such a bright little girl, and surely she's been off this island.

"I bet you've been to Campbell River. It's right over there." This time I gesture towards the easily-visible city across the channel.

"No, I don't think so."

"Well, have you been on the ferry?" I ask, pointing at the vessel now loading cars.

"I think so."

"Well, then you've been to Campbell River, because that's the only place it goes."

"Wow," she says with restrained surprise.

One of the reasons I'm not thrilled about places like this is because of the people on the dock. It's also one of the reasons I love these places.

* * * * *

THERE'S LITTLE TO PACK UP THIS MORNING, since the dinghy never went in the water and there's no anchor to deal with, so I'm quickly ready to go. The big seiner on the other side of the dock is now entertaining a half-dozen onboard visitors. The captain, who looks especially experienced, is showing these people the nets and the huge hydraulic drum used to deploy it. His visitors are definitely not locals. I hear some of their questions, and I can tell they know little about boats, but they're enjoying the tour. Unfortunately, they're so close that I'm sure I'll be a spectacle when I depart in front of them.

As I unhook my lines, a bearded man steps off the seiner, and watches intently, as if he's never seen a boat get underway before. I ignore him, and quickly prepare for departure. By now, the captain's seiner lesson has stopped, and all are watching me. My engines are running, and everyone is waiting for something to happen. The captain and all of his visitors have stepped off their boat, and are standing within a few metres of the Bayliner, watching.

This is a fairly tight spot, with fishing boats both in front and behind me, and a crowded dock on the other side of the narrow waterway. I'm facing in towards shore, so I'll have to cast off, turn around, and make a professional exit. Or maybe I should push off, and try to back out. Either scenario is going to tax my skills, but I'll take it slow and safe. Except everyone is watching.

As I step aboard the aft deck, I push off the dock with my foot, and climb up to the command bridge where the engines are idling in neutral. When I glance towards the small crowd, I notice the captain telling the bearded man something. Maybe he's saying: "Look, he's gonna' have to turn around now."

I slip the starboard throttle into reverse, wait a few seconds, and then push the port throttle into forward. The Bayliner slowly backs away from the dock as if I know what I'm doing. Leaving the throttles as they are, the boat pivots around like magic, and is now facing straight out the waterway. I glance to my left, and the captain is saying something to the bearded man again. Maybe: "That guy really knows what he's doing."

It's an amazing feat of seamanship I didn't think I could muster. And it won't happen every time I depart a dock (and less often when others are watching). But this big (to me) boat is a vessel I can handle. In fact, I'm starting to love it.

* * * * *

THE REST OF THE TRIP IS A JOY. I do some fishing on my way to Cortes Island, catching a 3-pound ling cod in the tidal rips near the Cape Mudge lighthouse. I'm using a Deep Six sinker and a Cop Car spoon with no flasher, since today the downrigger motor fails to operate, probably a victim of last winter's inactivity. I continue trolling across Wilby Shoal, just east of Cape Mudge, but catch nothing more. When you fish like I do, the joy is in the process rather than the size or quantity of the fish.

I spend another peaceful night on the hook at Manson's Landing, where there's plenty of room to swing near the shore in 40 feet of water. The sun continues to shine, and the air stays warm during the day and wonderfully cool at night. I briefly consider taking the dinghy to shore here, but there's really no reason to do so, so I just keep swinging on anchor.

Then, after a total of 5 days on the water (including only a few hours on land, if you don't count my dock time at Quathiaski Cove), I'll take my big boat back to Powell River. When I enter the breakwater at North Harbour, I'll slip in confidently, and swing my boat around using one throttle in forward and one in reverse, until I bump up gently against the dock. I'll leave a lot of the things that I hauled down to the boat last week right where they are, for this is only the beginning of the cruising season, and I'll be out on the chuck again very soon.

Then I'll go back up the lake and float around contentedly some more, enjoying what seems like an endless summer.

Epilogue

Inlets and More Inlets

There was a time when I thought my boating adventures would never be complete without a trip to the northern destinations I've read about in *A Curve in Time*, places with names like Minstrel Island and Knight Inlet. Originally, that was the purpose of this book, to bring readers to those places I've dreamed about.

But things change. Life throws curves, many of which are for the better. I still hope to visit the many places I intended to when I began this book. But as I wrote *Up the Inlet*, my goals changed. Thus, I've returned to many of the magnificent boating destinations that feed my soul, while discovering some new ones, too. If you love certain destinations, it's okay to keep enjoying them.

Halcyon Days was like that, too. There was a time, not so long ago, when I couldn't imagine another boat, for she seemed perfect. She is now enjoying her "retirement" on Powell Lake, where she serves as my alternate transportation to town when water conditions are rough, along with an occasional overnight cruise on the lake. As seasons passed, I nurtured dreams of a bigger boat on the chuck, with twin engines, and a dinghy bigger than *Mr. Bathtub* (who now goes for an occasional outing on Powell Lake).

To discover new locations, you have to momentarily sacrifice your precious time at old retreats. It's a tradeoff we face in all facets of life. There's good and there's more good, which makes decisions easier to accept.

The familiarity of old places leads to peace of mind, like the kind I feel when anchored at my favourite spot in Theodosia Inlet. Wherever you go, boating is like that. Time momentarily stops, while we dream of what might be up the next inlet. Then we retrieve our anchor and head home, already planning our next voyage.

I'll make it to Minstrel Island and Knight Inlet—someday. But until then, you'll find me cruising the northern Strait of Georgia. For adventures await us around every corner.

◊ ◊ ◊ ◊ ◊ ◊

Geographic Index

Anacortes, Washington p.168
Belllingham, Washington p.43, 56, 69, 71, 76-78, 96, 108, 116-117,140, 166, 168
Big Bay p.43, 46, 49
Blind Channel p.43, 47
Blubber Bay p.57, 118, 156-157, 159-160
Bowen Islanad p.102
Broughton Archipelago p.10, 21, 35, 37, 43, 48, 50-51, 137, 184, 185
Campbell River p.19, 37-38, 186, 194-195, 197, 199, 201
Cape Mudge p.196, 203
Chatham Point p.48
Chuckanut Bay, Washington p.71
Copeland Islands p.40-41, 65
Cortes Bay p.126-129
Cortes Island p.10, 49, 137, 203
Cottonwood Cove, Arizona p.87
Coward's Cove p.101
Deception Pass p.140-143, 145, 148, 166, 168-169, 172
Dent Island p.46, 49
Discovery Passage p.196-197
Drew Harbour p.12-13, 15, 36-37, 186-187, 192, 194
Egmont p.21-24, 32
False Creek p.86
Frances Bay p.44-46
Fraser River p.78, 80, 84-86, 90, 94-96, 98-99, 101, 110
Friday Harbor, Washington p.71, 73, 167, 170
Gibsons p.102
Gillard Passage p.46, 49
Grant's Reef p.35
Green Point p.47
Grief Point p.105

Geographic Index

Harwood Island p.52, 135-136, 164
Hernando Island p.35
Heriot Bay p.
Iron Mines p.
Johnstone Strait p.
LaConner, Washington p.
Lang Bay p.
Lewis Channel p.
Little Dent Island p.
Little North Beach, Washington p.
Lund p.Manson's Landing p.
Malaspina Strait p.56-57
Misery Bay p.25
Myrtle Rocks p.105
Mystery Reef p.35
Mitlenatch Island p.10, 12-16, 20, 35, 39-40, 200
Narrows Inlet p.25, 29-31
Pender Harbour p.105, 158
Porpoise Bay p.21, 23-24, 26-27
Quadra Island p.10, 12, 35, 38, 186-187, 195
Quathiaski Cove p.195, 197, 203
Rebecca Rock p.164
Rebbeca Spit p.10, 12-14, 36, 186-188
Refuge Cove p.43-44, 46, 49
Richmond, BC p.78-80, 84, 94-97, 110
River Rock Marina p.89
Rosario Strait, Washington p.71
Salmon Inlet p.21-22, 25-26, 29
San Juan Islands, Washington p.69, 71
Savary Island p.35, 125, 193
Scotch Fir Point p.32, 105
Sechelt Inlet p.21, 23-24, 27

Geographic Index

Secret Cove p.103
Sentry Shoal p.38-39
Seymour Narrows p.184, 199-200
Skookumchuck Narrows p.22, 24-25, 31-32
Spencer Spit, Washington p.71
Skyline Marina p.78, 80, 82, 86, 88
Swinomish Channel, Washington p.166, 168-169, 174, 176
Taku Resort, Drew Harbour p.192, 194
Texada Island p.56-57, 59, 62, 105, 108, 110-111, 114, 118-119, 122, 150-152, 154-156, 158-160
Thurston Bay p.48
Tofino Air Marina p.26-28
Tzoonie Narriws p.29-31
Van Anda p.56-57, 59, 118, 156
Westview's North Harbour p.34-35, 55, 68, 84, 94, 130, 138, 163, 185, 203
Wilby Shoals p.203
Willingdon Beach p.62, 105, 122
Yuculta Rapids p.43-44, 46, 49

About the Author

From 1980 to 2005, Wayne Lutz was Chairman of the Aeronautics Department at Mount San Antonio College in Los Angeles. He also served 20 years as a U.S. Air Force C-130 aircraft maintenance officer. His educational background includes a B.S. degree in physics from the University of Buffalo and an M.S. in systems management from the University of Southern California. The author is a flight instructor with 7000 hours of flying experience.

For the past three decades, he has spent summers in Canada, exploring remote regions in his Piper Arrow, camping next to his airplane. The author resides in a floating cabin on Canada's Powell Lake in all seasons, and occasionally in a city-folk condo in Bellingham, Washington. His writing genres include regional Canadian publications and science fiction.

Books by Wayne J. Lutz

Coastal British Columbia Stories
Up the Lake
Up the Main
Up the Winter Trail
Up the Strait
Up the Airway
Farther Up the Lake
Farther Up the Main
Farther Up the Strait
Cabin Number 5
Off the Grid
Up the Inlet

Science Fiction Titles
Across the Galactic Sea
Echo of a Distant Planet
Inbound to Earth
When Galazies Collide

Pacific Northwest Series
Flying the Pacific Northwest
Paddling the Pacific Northwest

www.PowellRiverBooks.com

www.ingramcontent.com/pod-product-compliance
Lightning Source LLC
Chambersburg PA
CBHW071732080526
44588CB00013B/1992